The 7-Second CV

The 7-Second CV

How to Land the Interview

JAMES REED

1 3 5 7 9 10 8 6 4 2

Published in 2019 by Virgin Books,
an imprint of Ebury Publishing,
20 Vauxhall Bridge Road,
London SW1V 2SA

Virgin Books is part of the Penguin Random House group of companies
whose addresses can be found at global.penguinrandomhouse.com

Penguin
Random House
UK

Cover Design: Hugh Adams
First published by Virgin Books in 2019

www.penguin.co.uk

A CIP catalogue record for this book is available from the British Library

ISBN 9780753553077

Typeset in 10.25/15pt Georgia Pro
by Integra Software Services Pvt. Ltd

Printed and bound in Great Britain by Clays Ltd, Elcograf S.p.A.

Penguin Random House is committed to a
sustainable future for our business, our readers
and our planet. This book is made from Forest
Stewardship Council® certified paper.

For the 'Super You'

James Reed is the Chairman of REED – Britain's biggest and best-known recruitment brand and the largest family-owned recruitment company in the world. James is a regular media commentator on work and labour market issues, with recent appearances including BBC News, Sky News, BBC Radio 2 and *The Apprentice*.

James is a best-selling author of two books, *Why You? 101 Interview Questions You'll Never Fear Again* and *Put Your Mindset to Work*, which he co-authored with Dr. Paul Stoltz.

James lives in London with his wife Nicola and their six children.

Contents

CHAPTER 1

What Recruiters Want

'You never get a second chance to make a first impression'
HEAD AND SHOULDERS TV COMMERCIAL

Seven seconds is all the time a recruiter will give your CV before it goes into the 'interview' or 'reject' pile – that's less time than it takes to cross the street, check your email, or take the rubbish out. Even a TV commercial has longer to grab your attention. The good news is that writing an attention-grabbing CV that lands you the interview is something you can learn. This book will tell you how. But first, why does every second count?

These days Britain is blessed with some of the best Olympic rowing teams in the world, but it wasn't always the case. Back in 1998, the GB Men's Rowing Eight was failing even to reach the finals of regattas. Losing race after race, they were desperate to win gold at the forthcoming Sydney Olympics, even though this seemed an impossible dream at the time. They realised that to be victorious they had to face their problems head on. They had to radically change how they trained. This led them to focus purely on performance, both professionally and personally. If a certain activity helped them to increase their rowing speed, they

1

did more of it. If it hindered it, they dropped it like a stone. And to help them decide which was which, they asked themselves one simple question: 'Will it make the boat go faster?' Because winning a race is all about timing – if you're only a fraction slower than your rival, you've lost. Every second counts.

Over the next 18 months they overcame challenge after challenge. They couldn't afford quality equipment, so they raised extra funds to buy it. Their focus needed improvement, so they developed an unshakeable belief that they could win. Most importantly, they encouraged an appetite for taking manageable risks, with the result that in the Olympic final they employed a strategy that they had only come up with the day before. Instead of the classic combination of a fast start and then a sprint at the end, they sprinted the whole way through. It was a bold move and it paid off: after years of defeats, they won gold. One of the crew, Ben Hunt-Davis, co-authored a book about this journey called *Will it Make the Boat Go Faster?* In it you can see the enormous effort that goes into shaving seconds off a race. Precious moments that make the difference between winning and losing.

Take away the Olympic medal and replace it with an interview offer, and that's what it's like when you write your CV. You're in a competition too, but this time to win the attention of a time-pressed recruiter who's been charged with scanning hundreds of CVs and has to decide who to award a coveted interview. Put yourself in the shoes of this person for a moment. Imagine it's your morning commute and the train is packed as usual. Knowing that you're going to be in interviews for most of the day, you decide to be proactive by tapping the email app on your phone and opening the CV attachments that have arrived the evening before. Scrolling down the top few lines of each, you drag them swiftly into 'yes' and 'no' folders and promise yourself you'll review the 'maybes' later. Except you don't, because when you finally return to your desk at lunchtime, another 50 have arrived. An alternative scenario is that automated software scans the CVs in advance of our human recruiter, but this delivers the same result.

This book shows you how to grab a hiring manager's attention. The seven-second rule might seem pretty dispiriting, but it doesn't have to be. In fact, it can be to your advantage, because success with your CV comes down to knowing what recruiters want. As soon as you know what it's like for them, you're on the first step to writing the CV that wins you the interview. This book will show you how to think of your CV not as a summary of your life (the common mistake many jobseekers make), but as a marketing document designed to attract employers to you.

> *'People have this brainwashed view that you have to write that you're a hardworking individual who works well with others, but you can actually read the same thing 10,000 times.'*

WHAT DO RECRUITERS WANT? I ASKED THEM

It turns out that recruiters are a pretty reasonable bunch and their needs are few. They want your CV to:

- Tell them up front why you're one of the best candidates for that particular job
- Be clear and easy to read so they can compare it instantly with other CVs
- Bring out your mindset and personality

> *'Read the job spec and have it next to your CV and ask yourself if they match. If they don't, would you interview that person? Lay out your CV in a way that reflects what the recruiter wants and you can change it relatively easily.'*

I know this is what recruiters want, because I've asked them. I'm fortunate enough to be Chairman of the Reed Group, the UK's best-known recruiter, which gives me access to around 12,000 employers advertising their vacancies on reed.co.uk every day. Not only that, at Reed we have our own network of 2,000 recruitment consultants, who work both with companies that are searching for people and with people who are looking for new positions. This gives them a valuable understanding not only into what recruiters want from a CV, but also into the elements that jobseekers find most difficult to write about. By surveying recruiters via our site, and by travelling up and down the country talking to our in-house recruitment specialists, I have a clear picture of what goes on inside a recruiter's head. In other words, not what you might think that they're after, but what they actually put into practice when they open the CVs that are sent to them. At the same time, I surveyed the job hunters who browse the 250,000-plus roles on our website every day. I quizzed them on what they thought were the most important elements of a CV, and how they went about writing one. This has given me a unique insight into the problems you might be grappling with when you go about crafting your CV.

'I think some people genuinely don't know how to write a CV, or don't know where to start.'

So what did I learn? It turns out that what recruiters think most makes a CV stand out is relevant work history, closely followed by a clear visual layout that's easy to read. However, spelling mistakes and frequent job changes are likely to land it in the reject pile. A quarter of hiring managers use Applicant Tracking Systems to screen CVs, and three-quarters prefer a CV to be two pages long (if printed out, double-sided is best). According to them, you're also advised to use a reverse-chronological format, to include a cover letter, and to be prepared for your social media profiles to be scrutinised.

Collating all these discoveries together led me to create what I call 'The Fatal Five', or the five key mistakes that could land your CV in the reject pile. They are, in order of importance:

1. A lack of relevant work history
2. Spelling mistakes
3. Frequent job changes
4. Not enough information
5. Poor visual layout

You'll learn how to avoid these problems, and also to highlight your strengths, as you go through this book.

HOW I WROTE THIS BOOK

As you've already seen, in this book you'll read many of the pearls of wisdom my recruiters have given me in the form of quotes sprinkled liberally throughout. In fact, I went even further afield to source some of them, by asking my wider business contacts for their own experiences of fielding and screening CVs. Some of the mistakes they told me about were pretty eye-opening. One even had a candidate apply for a position, and instead of attaching their CV, they'd mistakenly replaced it with a court summons for their upcoming trial for fraud and misrepresentation. Then there was this one:

'Failing to turn off "track changes" and having various editors'/friends'/family contributions and notes all over the Word document. It was a CV for an IT role.'

Or how about this one?

> *'Someone applied for a job with me, and on their CV, under previous employment, they claimed to be doing my previous role while I was actually doing it myself.'*

You'll see that by including these quotes, this book is written in two voices. The first is mine: I am your guide and career coach and I've tried to keep it as lighthearted as possible (who wants to wade through a heavy-going book about CVs?). The second is the voice of the recruiters, which strikes a tougher tone. These people are the realists because they read CVs day in and day out, and you need to pay as much attention to them as to me. Even the humorous examples have a serious underlying message, because behind every CV howler there's a hopeful candidate who has likely been disappointed.

Over and above the way your CV is written and formatted lies an important goal: your CV must inspire trust, and inspire a recruiter to make that leap of faith by offering you an interview. Taking on a new person is always a risk for an employer, which means that CV mistakes and obvious exaggerations are a huge turn-off. On the other hand, there are plenty of ways you can present yourself as the most credible candidate for the job.

WHAT IS A JOB, ANYWAY?

Your CV has one purpose and one purpose only: to win you an interview. That means that it should convince the person reading it that you have the ability to do that particular job better than any of the other applicants.

> *'People think that a CV is going to get you a job. Well, actually it isn't. A CV has a limited purpose and that's to get you in the interview seat.'*

But what is 'that particular job'? At this point it's worth considering what a job actually is. Contrary to what you may have assumed, it's not a set of tasks, duties, or even responsibilities, although it can involve all three. Think back to when a company is first founded. An ambitious entrepreneur thinks they can sell something more cheaply, or of a higher quality, than their competitors, and a new business is born. Soon they find themselves with more to do than they have time for, which creates a set of further issues and gives the owner a headache, so they hire staff to clear those worries off their plate. And that's what a job is: a problem to be solved. If your CV can show, within seven seconds of opening it, why you're a person who can solve their problem quickly, professionally, and skilfully, you're in with a strong chance of being offered an interview.

SUPER YOU!

Picture this, you're the star of a new movie called *Super You*. Your name is in lights and your image is emblazoned across the promotional posters. You're looking sharp and your smile lets the world know that you have got what it takes. You mean business.

We are fantasising, of course, but to an employer your superpower is whatever makes you more outstanding for the job than anyone else – in other words, your unique selling point. Do you know what yours is? Because if you don't, how will they? When a recruiter opens up the stash of CVs in their inbox, they usually have a good idea of the mix of skills, talents, and experience they're looking for. It might be that they're after someone who's organised, experienced with numbers, and confident enough to challenge people around the business. If you're a natural with figures and highly efficient, this special combination of characteristics could be your superpower. Or it could be that they want a self-starter who relishes the prospect of creating a new project out of nothing. If you enjoy being left to 'get on with it' in your current role, and work better unsupervised than with constant support, your superpower would be ideal for them.

'Make sure you put your unique selling point across. What did you do in your last role? What made you stand out? How did you impact your most recent business? And how will you plan to carry that across to your next role?'

'Super You' is you at your best. It's you when you're right for the job. And it's you when your CV is based on your special talents, skills, and experience. Owning your superpower means that you're in the ideal position to pick the right job to apply for, and then to describe it in your CV so that it zooms straight to the heart of what the recruiter is seeking.

YOUR 3G MINDSET

You should think of your mindset as the 'X factor' in applying for jobs, partly because it's necessary in developing the resilience for the process, and partly because it's what employers nowadays are looking for. When surveyed, 97 per cent of hiring managers said that they would employ someone with the right mindset ahead of someone with the right skills, because they know that the nature of jobs is changing so quickly – experience gained one year may be out of date the next. They'd therefore prefer a candidate who exhibits the following mindset traits, which I call the 3Gs:

- *Global* – this is about being able to see beyond the horizon and understand the big-picture implications of what you do. Key words for your CV to show you have this are: adaptable, flexible, collaborative, open, and innovative.
- *Good* – this is about ensuring that your approach is for the benefit of all, so that the impact you have is positive for those

around you and your organisation. Key words for your CV to show you have this are: loyal, sincere, trusted, kind, and fair.

- *Grit* – this is about having the tenacity and resilience to keep achieving your goals, despite setbacks and adversity. Key words for your CV to show you have this are: committed, accountable, determined, driven, and energetic.

'If you go through a CV and think the person is engaging and enthusiastic or personable (as much as you can gauge from a piece of paper), then you're going to want to give them a call and speak to them.'

You may have spotted a contradiction here. Employers *say* that they often hold the 3Gs as being more important than experience and skills, while the recruiters we surveyed assert that relevant work history is the most coveted quality in a CV. In the answer to this conundrum lies the essence of a successful CV. The fact is that hiring managers want both, so your challenge is to show that you have a winning 3G mindset *and* the right experience, in equal measure.

HOW TO USE THIS BOOK

The next four chapters contain the fundamentals of CV writing, and are ones you should definitely read before you progress any further. Crafting a CV that survives the seven-second test, and then engages a recruiter to the end, means being confident about the basics – even if you think you know them already. When you go through these chapters you'll almost certainly come across something new that you haven't thought of before.

After that, you can pick and choose according to your needs. If you're worried you have a particular issue that will look bad on your CV, such as gaps in your work history or a lack of relevant experience, Chapter 6 will help you solve that problem. If you're applying for a job in the professions, the creative industries, or in academia or research, you'll want to check out Chapter 7. And if you'd like to learn how to stand out with your personal brand and how to impress recruiters online, you'd be highly recommended to read Chapter 8.

Make sure that you use the crowdsourced wisdom in this book in whatever way you can to create a CV that stands out.

CHAPTER 2

Make a Flying Start

CV stands for Curriculum Vitae, which can be loosely translated as 'the course of one's life'. You'll not be including every element of your personal history in your CV, but you need to state the obvious elements such as your name, contact details, education, and work history. Without these solid foundations in place, none of the other amazing things you can do with your CV will work. It's a bit like papering a wall without filling in the cracks – you'll have the satisfaction of a fast finished result, but it won't take long for the weaknesses to show through. What's more, you don't want to write just any old CV. You want to create one that is personal to you, survives the seven seconds a recruiter will give it, and will help you to stand out and give you the edge. This chapter and the next will give you the tools to lay your foundations securely so you can do just that.

ROGUES' GALLERY OF JOBSEEKERS

Before we begin in earnest, though, let's take a tongue-in-cheek look at the various types of jobseeker (and their CVs) that can be spotted in the wild by any recruiter with a decent pair of binoculars. Can you pick yourself out of this list?

The spray and pray

Characteristics: A spammer, sends the same CV to every job advert that seems remotely applicable to them, often multiple times a day.

Good points: By the law of averages, they may strike lucky.

Bad points: Due to their indiscriminate approach, they're unlikely to win the job they really want (assuming that they know what it is) and are highly likely to be disappointed.

Improvement tactics: Applying for jobs isn't like tossing coins into a fountain and hoping one of them will bring you luck. Employers want to feel special, and your CV should make them think that their job is the only one in the world you'd really love to do. Even more importantly, you need to show you could do it better than anyone else who applies, and an indiscriminate approach won't give you the chance to do that. So stop the mass emailing and start to be more selective.

The undercover agent

Characteristics: Feels embarrassed about promoting their achievements, hiding them so skilfully in their CV it ends up resembling an undercover exercise that would make MI5 proud.

Good points: Few. The only benefit of this approach is that it won't come across as arrogant.

Bad points: Many. Most recruiters don't have the time to excavate a candidate's most valuable qualities – they want to be told up front.

Improvement tactics: Value yourself. If you don't know what makes you fantastic, how do you expect a recruiter to? Be bold in your writing. Highlight your skills and achievements in your CV, and be specific about them. Spies aren't usually allowed to talk about their work, but this is the one place where being boastful is almost compulsory.

The butterfly

Characteristics: Has had more jobs than they've had hot dinners, resulting in a CV resembling the inventory at a pick 'n' mix stall.

Good points: Their experience is diverse – in fact, there's pretty much nothing they've not tried their hand at. They're also great at applying for, and being offered, the jobs they want (or they wouldn't have had so many).

Bad points: They've never stayed long enough in one role to prove their worth, so have few substantial achievements to shout about in their CV. They can also appear unfocused.

Improvement tactics: You can't turn back the clock, but consider doing some soul searching about what you really want to do before you apply for yet another job. In the meantime, consider a skills-based CV format, rather than listing your jobs individually. And be ready to explain in your cover letter why you've been a job hopper – there may be perfectly acceptable reasons why this is the case. If there aren't, you can always blame it on the vagaries of youth.

Pinocchio

Characteristics: Literally too good to be true. Has already done absolutely everything the job requires, and has the credentials and qualifications to 'prove' it. What's more, they've achieved world peace in their spare time.

Good points: None.

Bad points: They're about to be rumbled, which can be seriously bad news. Fraudulent misrepresentation isn't something you want to have on your record.

Improvement tactics: Take out the lies – you'll only feel a fool in the interview when you have to justify yourself, or later when you're fired. And while you're about it, try valuing your real achievements and skills more highly. Most of the time, people only falsify their credentials when they don't think the real thing is adequate. If that's genuinely the case you'll need to adjust your expectations, but if not, a positively worded CV based on facts is the best route.

The artist

Characteristics: Considers the common or garden CV to be beyond boring, and favours festooning the document with colourful fonts, graphics, images, and interactive video clips.

Good points: Impossible to ignore.

Bad points: The hiring manager needs a pair of sunglasses to read it.

Improvement tactics: Unless you're going for a graphic-design role (in which case, make sure your design is tasteful), cut out the fancy stuff. You want the person reading your CV to have a quick sense of what makes you special, rather than to click 'delete' because you've given them a headache. There's no need for visual bells and whistles in order to stand out – that's what your unique personality and achievements are for.

The newbie

Characteristics: Has just left school, with no work history beyond cleaning cars for the neighbours. Big dreams, small credentials.

Good points: They're young, energetic, and grateful for any chance to prove themselves. Also, as shown in my book *Put Your Mindset to Work*, 97 per cent of employers pick mindset over skill set.

Bad points: A recruiter has to take a massive punt on whether they're worth interviewing or not, because the recruiter doesn't have much to go on.

Improvement tactics: Make the most of your qualifications and achievements at school, and focus on your mindset. Show you know what you're aiming at and how you plan to contribute to the company.

The narcissist

Characteristics: Wildly ambitious, with dreams overshooting their experience or ability. Sees pleas to listen to reason as a personal affront.

Good points: There's no hiding their light under a bushel for them, which means they're often offered an interview.

Bad points: An inexperienced or ineffective interviewer can sometimes be swayed into offering them a job, to the detriment of everyone they're about to work with. Chaos and resignations ensue.

Improvement tactics: If this is you, you're unlikely to be reading a book giving you advice on your CV (or, indeed, on anything). So let's assume that you can skip this one.

The Emmental

Characteristics: Loves nothing more than a long break between jobs, either by choice or necessity. This results in a CV with more holes than a chunk of Swiss cheese.

Good points: Given work appears to be optional, the recruiter can feel confident this candidate has made a positive decision to apply for the role.

Bad points: Repeatedly leaving jobs without another to go to can appear at best unreliable, and at worst suspicious.

Improvement tactics: Any recruiter will want to know 'why the holes?' You may have perfectly good reasons for them: taking on caring responsibilities, an unexpected family crisis, or a one-off difficult experience in a company are acceptable examples. The worst thing you can do is to try to hide them, because any experienced employer will sniff them out. Put the dates for the gaps in your CV and give reasons for them – you may have gained some valuable skills during those fallow periods, after all.

The shape shifter

Characteristics: Seeks a move into a different industry or role type, rather than the standard upgrade from their current job. This can involve moving up a level, career switching, and even downshifting.

Good points: They're not going for the easy option, so a recruiter can see that they want the job and have given it serious consideration.

Bad points: They're hard to offer an interview to, because their work history doesn't fit the sort of pattern that leads directly to the role on offer.

Improvement tactics: Think of your CV from a recruiter's perspective. You'll be up against candidates with way more relevant experience than you, so give some thought to what format you use. Stacked in your favour are your transferable skills, so position them high up and explain in your personal statement what has led you to this shift.

The digital devotee

Characteristics: Scoffs at the traditional, written CV as being prehistoric. Instead, has multiple websites, social media profiles, and blogs. Owns more urls than undergarments.

Good points: For the right type of role, such as in digital marketing or IT, this approach can work. And this candidate certainly shows they're not afraid to innovate or move with the times.

Bad points: The 'digital only' approach doesn't tend to be what a recruiter wants, because it's not convenient. Like most of us, the digital devotee doesn't like having their expectations rudely disrupted by someone thinking they know better.

Improvement tactics: There's nothing wrong with supplementing your CV with a well-thought-through digital presence – in fact it can help you. But don't throw the baby out with the bathwater. Unless the job advert specifies otherwise, you're going to have to buckle down and write a CV just like your parents did. Even if it kills you.

... and finally ...

The sharp shooter

Characteristics: Creates the CV that's perfect for the job, and sends it with a motivational cover letter to exactly the right person.

Good points: Sees their side of the bargain as showing why they'd add value to the organisation.

Bad points: Rarely spotted in the wild (although that certainly helps them stand out when they're caught in the recruiter's sights).

Improvement tactics: If this is you, you've obviously read this book already.

YOUR CV BASICS

Let's get the first steps out of the way, so that you're confident you're starting on the right foot. Here's what to include:

Your name and contact details. Yes, this is obvious. But believe it or not, there are jobseekers who forget that a recruiter needs to be able to get in touch with a jobseeker if they like what they see. So add your full name (first name and surname, there's no need to include Mr or Mrs), address, and a way of being contacted. Give an email address and phone number (if you're happy to be called and you'll be able to answer it – you don't want the recruiter to have to leave more than one voicemail). Bonus tip: nothing says 'I job hunt on my boss's time' like using your work email address.

> *'I'm surprised at how open some people are about listing potentially inappropriate email addresses in their contact information, such as sausagedog81@hotmail.com.'*

Your social media accounts and/or personal website. There are pros and cons to adding social media details into your CV, and we'll go through them in Chapter 8. For now, just be aware that you may want to include these at the end.

Hobbies and interests. These are good to include because while your work history and qualifications tell the story of your head, your hobbies and interests tell the story of your heart. In other words, what you choose to do in your spare time can be more revealing than what you have to do at work. They also offer useful talking points and common interests for your interview, and demonstrate the mindset qualities of Good, Global, and Grit that I explained on page 8. What's more, if you lack work history they can show your suitability in other ways. Having said all that, consider including them only if doing so achieves at least one of the following:

- Shows you have an aptitude for the specific role
- Helps you to stand out if you have an unusual hobby
- Illustrates your mindset qualities

> 'We had a CV once in which the candidate said she cleaned her car daily and had gravel in her driveway.'

Here are a few examples of interests and how they could relate to a role:

- Coding or programming (for a technology job)
- Fashion and beauty blogging (for journalists, copywriters, and fashion jobs)
- Sports and conditioning training (for personal trainers and jobs in sport)
- Being president of a society or club (for management positions)

- Cooking and baking (for jobs in the catering industry)
- Theatre and drama (for jobs in sales)
- Coaching a local football team (for jobs requiring leadership and motivation)

Hobbies and interests are subjective – one person's passion is another's idea of hell, so consider how they might appear to someone who doesn't know you. Also, being specific makes them more believable and concrete. For instance, 'a weekly five-a-side football game with friends' is not as compelling as, 'I successfully organised a range of regional five-a-side football tournaments, including managing the bookings, venues, and participants'. And always put your hobbies and interests at the end of your CV – they're there to seal the deal, not as a key selling point.

> *'I once received a CV for a cinema manager position and in the hobbies and interests section the applicant said that "he liked to handle guns".'*

On the other hand, if you don't think you have any hobbies or interests worth mentioning, don't put 'socialising with friends' or 'going to the cinema'. These won't add value to your CV, so you're better off leaving this section out entirely. But do consider taking up some volunteering or involving yourself in your community – it's a great hobby and a way of showing you can be a committed team player.

> *'I ask candidates to list their hobbies and interests then tell me what they say about them. For example, if you're a rock climber, that may mean you're a risk taker.'*

> *'Under interests and achievements, someone wrote that they had "potentially swum with saltwater crocodiles". It was the "potentially" part that made me giggle.'*

THE BASICS TO LEAVE OUT

We have all experienced oversharing. There is even a hashtag used to indicate that someone has provided an excessive amount of personal information, #TMI (too much information). When writing your CV you need to include just enough information to put your message across successfully, but not so much that you distract the reader from the main event. This means that there are a few elements that you should definitely leave out:

Your marital status. This isn't relevant and to include it could be considered odd.

Your religion. Unless you're applying for a religious role, this isn't one to include. It could alienate or even offend the recruiter, and you don't want to give the impression you're intending to bring your beliefs into your workplace or job (however unfair that may seem).

Your age, gender, sexual orientation, and ethnicity. It's illegal for an employer to discriminate according to these, so they'd rather you leave this information out.

Now you know the obvious details to include and remove, let's look at the other main areas a recruiter will be interested in: your skills, work history, education, and qualifications.

GATHERING YOUR IRRESISTIBLE INGREDIENTS

Writing your CV is a bit like making a cake. You need your ingredients to hand before you begin (that's your skills, experience, and qualifications), so that you can mix them together in the right order (that's your CV format). After that, you put it in the oven to bake (that's your checking and proofreading) and finally you decorate it so it's tempting and delicious (that's your tailoring). At the end you will have a CV to share with whoever may be most attracted by it, and that will definitely take just seven seconds to consume.

Tempting though it may be to dive into writing your CV straight away, it pays to gather the ingredients before you begin. If you don't do that, you run the risk of forgetting some key fact, or of overlooking a useful skill you didn't think you had. Also, you may become distracted if you have to hunt for key information part way through writing. Here's a checklist of the information you need:

- The key jobs you've done, together with dates
- Educational achievements and qualifications
- Work-related training and qualifications
- Your skills, split into hard and soft
- Your transferable skills

Let's look at each element in turn.

Your past and current jobs. Not surprisingly, recruiters want to know what you've already done so they can judge whether you have the right experience for the job on offer. Even apart from this, your employment history says a lot about you: what you enjoy (and don't enjoy), how long you tend to stick around in a company, and what you're good at. So dredge your memory, look through old CVs, ask your friends and family if you need to, and come up with a list of all the jobs you've done since you left school (or even while you were there, if you're a recent leaver). You don't need the exact date of starting and leaving – the month and year are usually sufficient.

When I asked hiring managers what was the most important factor for making a CV stand out, they said one thing loud and clear: relevant work history. This means that the way you present your work history must explain how you've already done, or are prepared to do, what they're looking for. This isn't always easy even when you have the right experience, but when you haven't it can feel downright dispiriting. There are various clever ways of tackling this issue, and we'll look at them not only in this chapter but also in Chapter 6.

> *'Including reasons for leaving can be a good idea if you've done a lot of contract work, as you don't want people to think you're a job hopper.'*

What if you've not been working for long? You might be worried that your job history will look a bit bare. But remember, what you do outside of work can have as much of an impact on a recruiter as what you do in it – it says a lot about you as a person and shows initiative and commitment. You can include these elements even if you have a long work history, of course, but they're particularly useful if you have some space to fill. Think about what you can contribute from these areas of your life:

Volunteer work. This could be helping out in your local community, volunteering for a charity, or even manning the cake stall at your school fair. If you can show commitment and leadership, teamwork, or project management skills, it's worth including. Also, pinpoint your major accomplishments and what you learned during your involvement – these could be great ingredients for your skills section.

Hobbies and interests. As mentioned earlier, if you can show how these are relevant to the job you're applying for, they can be a helpful way of rounding out your CV.

> *'Someone applied for a post as a researcher to a Tory MP, proudly telling me how long they'd been a member of the Labour Party.'*

Major life experiences. Studying abroad, having a side job, writing a blog, or running a part-time business – these can all show your personal qualities. That eBay habit of yours could be a substitute for business work history if you've made a profit on what you've sold. Or what about your Duke of Edinburgh Award? What did that teach you?

Your education, training, and qualifications. Split these into those that are 'general' and those that are directly related to the role you're applying for. Make sure you have specifics such as dates and grades, as well as any special awards or extra courses you've been on.

> 'One of my favourite CV howlers: City In Gills instead of City and Guilds.'

Your hard skills. A hard skill is something you know, are trained in, or have an aptitude for – examples are creating a pivot table in Excel, driving a forklift truck, or managing projects using PRINCE2®. You'll notice these are objective skills, which means that someone watching you could see you were putting them into practice. It can be tricky to pull your own list of hard skills together because we tend to take for granted what we know, so give this one some serious thought. Think back on the jobs you've done, and jot down the knowledge that you gained in each. Then ask yourself: what type of work is always given to you because you're a safe pair of hands? What does your boss praise you for? What do your colleagues come to you for help with? What training courses have you been on? These will give you clues as to what hard skills you have.

Your soft skills. A soft skill is a bit like the elephant in the room: you just know it's there. Your soft skills affect how you do your

23

job, and examples are teamwork, leadership, time management, problem solving, and communication. They make a huge difference to being offered an interview, because they help to differentiate between you and other candidates. Employers don't just want someone who can do the job, they want someone who can rub along well with others, inspire them, and communicate effectively. In fact, you can think of your soft skills as being like the filling in your CV cake, binding together the solid layers to make a tempting whole.

Because they're not easy to observe they can be hard to pin down, and you'd not be the only candidate to figure you could fake your soft skills because no-one can prove whether you have them or not. Who'll know, right? Wrong. Tossing a random bunch of soft skills into your CV mix is a recipe for disaster, as recruiters are masters at ignoring them when they're vaguely presented without timescales, dates, or attachments to jobs or tasks. The best way to talk about them is with evidence based on your achievements, so while you're listing your soft skills, think about where you've proved that you've put them into practice. You also want to make sure that you don't appear self-contradictory. If you say you're great at working with people but are equally adept at operating alone, for instance, this might not come across as believable.

'There should be three things that are obvious in your key skills: the first is a number (five years' experience, for instance), the second is a name drop (where did you get that experience?), and the third is proof.'

Your transferable skills. These are skills you've developed in a previous role, that will help you succeed in the one you're applying for. They're the holy grail of skills, because you can use them to show that you can do a job for which you may not feel totally qualified. This widens your job search out like nothing else. You'll be amazed at how many of your skills are transferable, and here's a little exercise to work out which ones. First, list the hard and soft skills required by the job (look at the job advert for clues). Next, pick from the hard and soft skills you've already written down to create a list of those that would fit them. You'll have two lists looking like this:

Skills in job advert

My relevant, transferable skills

1. _____   1. _____
2. _____   2. _____
3. _____   3. _____
4. _____   4. _____
5. _____   5. _____

Be careful with this, though. Just because you have a skill, that doesn't mean it will transfer every time. For instance, if as a sales person you had to learn persuasion skills, that bodes well for a position involving one-to-one negotiation. What it doesn't mean is that you necessarily have the ability to lead a large team, however persuasive you might have to be to pull that off.

> 'One guy said he had "usurped" his manager.
> Maybe it's just me, but I'm not finding that a skill
> in high demand.'

A final word about skills. It can be easy, when you read the job description and see some basic skill requirements listed, to assume that's all they're after. And it may be, but think about the salary they're offering and the level of the role. Suppose the recruiter wants you to be 'proficient in Adobe InDesign'. You've been using it for a couple of months now, knocking out simple designs for your boss on a monthly basis, so you put 'InDesign experience' on your CV. But if you are expected to use it proficiently, this might include complex page templates and an extensive knowledge of the many typesetting features. Does the thought of that bring you out in a cold sweat? Listing skills on your CV means you're confident in them, so take out anything that you don't feel ready to talk about yet. Many interviewers carry out on-the-spot competency tests, at which point you'd better be sure that you really are 'fluent in French'.

Now you have all your ingredients to hand, it's time to prioritise them. Highlight the ones that are most relevant to the job or industry you're applying for and leave out the rest – you don't want to confuse the recruiter by throwing in the kitchen sink. Likewise, consider the sell-by date of some. If you're in your forties, your GCSE subjects are not relevant any more, nor is the Saturday job you had while you were at college. But if you're a school leaver, you'll want to include this information.

PASSING THE CONFIDENCE TEST

You'll have gathered by now that writing a CV demands a certain level of confidence in yourself. If you find this hard, remember that we all tend to underestimate ourselves. Take a feel for what you're capable of and add on 100 per cent. Forget (almost) everything you've heard about self-proclaimed greatness equalling arrogance, and accept that blowing your own trumpet is often the only way a recruiter will take note of your level of ambition – provided, of course, that your achievements are relevant, honest, and you don't go overboard. Remember: a hiring manager can't know how good you are unless you show them. You're 'Super You', not 'Any Old You'.

YOUR CV FORMAT

At last, it's time to take the information you've collected and work out which order to put it in. To do that you'll need a format to work with, and there are two main ones you can use: reverse-chronological and skills-based.

'I would always start a CV with some form of personal statement.'

Reverse-chronological: Most jobseekers use this format, which means listing your jobs from most recent to most distant, followed by your skills, achievements, education, and hobbies. Luckily, my research found that 88 per cent of recruiters prefer this format because it doesn't give candidates anywhere to hide. They can see exactly what you've done and when, and whether or not there are any gaps. For this reason it's great if you're applying for a job that's a natural progression from what you've done before, and if you haven't got any spaces in your employment history. It's less helpful if you're seeking a change in direction or if your job history is shot full of holes. Chapter 6 will look at how to help with this type of scenario so we won't go into detail here, but in the meantime let's look at an alternative format below that will help.

'I received a CV where they had copied a CV template from online and simply left the template as well as filled it in! The template writing was also bold red and very noticeable. I'm not sure how they managed that one.'

Skills-based: Sometimes called 'function-based' because it starts with your skills and particular aspects of your experience, and includes your work history only at the end of the document. It's helpful if you haven't had much time in the industry or type of job you're applying for, especially if you're trying to change career or turn a hobby or passion into a job. It can also work well if you've had several short-term positions, have gaps in your work history, or your previous jobs are so similar to each other that describing each one individually seems redundant. It places emphasis on your transferable skills, rather than on your previous jobs. However, for recruiters it's not ideal. Having your experience in chronological order makes it easy for them to see what you've done without having to piece it together themselves; some also worry they'll not spot gaps in your employment.

'It's better to do your CV in a reverse-chronological format for the simple reason that people will usually only read the first page.'

You can find templates for reverse-chronological and skills-based CVs on pages 166 and 168, and they will save you time and ensure that you're not making any basic mistakes. You can also download the documents themselves and work with them straight away, by visiting https://www.reed.co.uk/career-advice/cvs/cv-templates.

The downloads are great for helping you to stop procrastinating – they will make sure you don't find yourself fiddling with the margin sizes of your Word document for hours. After all, a load of white space on a screen can be daunting, especially if you haven't written a good CV in the past. If you're worried about using a template because you think it will make you look the same as everyone else, bear in mind that they're just a starting point. There are many different options to suit your skills and level of experience, so whether you've recently finished school, are looking for a graduate CV template, or need to explain a difficult career break, our templates will have you covered. And, as they're written by Reed's dedicated career-advice experts, you can be confident that they're logically formatted in a clear and concise way.

'You can tell a good CV straight away. It's clearly formatted with paragraphs. If I see one that's a big block

*of text, I'm not going to take the time to read through it
all, and nor is a hiring manager.'*

Now you know what format you're using, let's look at how to craft the content of your CV so that your best points spring off the page.

CHAPTER 3

Write Your CV

Over half of the jobseekers I surveyed said that they had sought help at some point with writing their CV, the most popular tactic being to ask a friend to look at it. I'm worried about the half that didn't ask. These applicants also revealed that their biggest challenge was writing their personal statement, which is something that we will cover later in this chapter. It's included last because it's easier to craft it once you've completed the rest of your CV (and not just because it's a good excuse to put it off).

DOING THE WRITING BIT

A super CV needs to be a concise and straightforward representation of the 'Super You'. This means that the way you write your CV has a major impact on whether it survives the seven-second recruiter test, and also on whether it keeps them reading to the end. So before we move into how to communicate your job history, qualifications, and skills, let's look first at some general writing tips that will make an enormous difference to how well your CV will be received.

Words to avoid

Here's what *not* to use.

- Long, passive phrases – they put the reader to sleep (more on them in a moment)

- Overly technical information and jargon, unless you're sure the recruiter will understand it
- Recruiters' pet hates, such as:
  - Goal-driven
  - Strong work ethic
  - Multi-tasker
  - Detail-oriented
  - Self-motivated

Why do hiring managers pass over these? Because they're clichés that they've read thousands of times before, and they don't really say a lot about you. Hands up if you know what a goal-driven, detail-oriented, multi-tasker actually is? Neither do recruiters. Sometimes, of course, you'll need to use these words, but make them more meaningful by expanding on why, and give examples of where you've shown these qualities. A recruiter doesn't just want to know that you're goal-driven, they want to be convinced by the evidence for it.

In the last chapter we touched on the importance of being a confident 'Super You', and why you're best assuming that you're more capable than you think you are. One way jobseekers can give themselves away in the confidence stakes is by overusing what are called 'qualifiers'. These are words such as 'quite', 'probably', 'sometimes', and 'possibly'. Try eliminating these words from your CV and see how that makes it more forthright. Don't focus on what you can't do but on what you can. Introductions like, 'Although I don't have much experience in ...' won't do you any favours. If you lack a skill or qualification for the job you're applying for, apologising isn't going to persuade the employer to consider you, and if it's not completely necessary, why mention it? Instead, draw attention to the skills and experiences that make you a good fit.

'"Quite" is a word that should never be in a CV.'

Words to use

So what should you write instead? It goes without saying that you should always be positive when describing yourself, which means using power words. Some examples of powerful ways to describe yourself are:

- Accurate
- Adaptable
- Caring
- Committed
- Confident
- Dependable
- Flexible
- Hard-working
- Innovative
- Pro-active
- Resilient
- Responsible

Again, make sure that you back them up with evidence by including them in your previous experience, responsibilities, accomplishments, and any targets you've hit.

> 'A good CV isn't just words, it's numbers as well. So in accountancy, if you put 3,000 invoices a month on a ledger, don't just write, "I completed the ledger", because you could be doing that for an SME in a team of one, or a blue chip company in a team of ten.'

Here are some power words you can use to describe what you've done, and you can find a longer list on page 183:

- Accomplished
- Achieved

- Completed
- Created
- Developed
- Formulated
- Generated
- Implemented
- Innovated
- Introduced
- Led
- Managed
- Negotiated
- Planned
- Produced
- Represented
- Secured
- Started

Again, how you use these words is as important as the ones you choose in the first place. Formulate strong statements that demonstrate your skills and experience in action, using terms that show you are positive and proactive. Flimsy phrases such as, 'Attempted to improve internal communications' won't get you an interview. And finally, always use the active, rather than the passive, voice. Here's the difference:

Passive voice: 'I am considered to be an excellent communicator.'

Active voice: 'I am an excellent communicator.'

The active voice is more concise and impactful, helping your CV to pass the seven-second test. And, of course, in a real CV you'd back up your claim to be an excellent communicator with an impressive, specific example.

Putting it all together

Now you know the words to avoid and to use, let's start stringing them together into effective sentences, each headed up with a bullet point. Instead of writing, 'Responsible for IT strategy and team meetings', swap this for 'Created a team of diverse IT professionals to develop innovative solutions for our most persistent IT problems'. Or instead of writing, 'Supervised customer service team for retail operations', swap this for 'Co-ordinated and led the customer service team to improve satisfaction rates by 29 per cent in six months, by harvesting best practices from unrelated industries'. Can you see how you're making use of your power words?

Next, consider which of your bullet points are the most important, and put them in order. Hiring managers will skim downwards rather than reading them in detail, so you want to have the key information up top. Take this example from an IT manager's CV:

- Led an IT project involving five stakeholders which reduced marketing costs by 17 per cent
- Worked with HR team to improve absentee reporting

The first bullet is more impressive because it's specific, shows leadership skills, and highlights the financial benefit to the business. The second, while also good, doesn't showcase the applicant's achievements as highly. To decide how to order your bullets, ask yourself: if the hiring manager could only read two on your list, which would you choose?

'To see if a candidate's CV passes the seven-second test, I get them to turn it over so they can't see it. Then I ask them to turn it back over, look at it for seven seconds, and then write down everything about themselves that

> *they just read. We look at what they've got and I ask them, "Does that make you the number one candidate for the job?" Often they say no, so I tell them, "Well, if you wouldn't give the job to yourself, what makes you think that a recruiter would?"'*

And finally, write in the first person, not the third. That means saying 'I' not 'he' or 'she'. It's less common for people to make this mistake nowadays, but the last thing a recruiter wants to read is, 'Sheila Jones is an experienced sales person'. Instead, they want to see, 'I'm an experienced sales person'. It's more personal and direct.

Let's summarise with some handy dos and don'ts for writing your CV.

CV-writing dos

- The most effective CVs aren't just informative, they're also concise. Try to get straight to the most pertinent points so you don't take up more than two sides of A4 – in my research with recruiters, 75 per cent say they prefer that length. If you're printing it, do it double-sided so it takes up one sheet of paper.
- Use bullet points. They're a great way to draw attention to key facts or relevant information, allowing a hiring manager to skim the document without having to hack through chunks of text. For every bullet you write, include an action and a result. For instance, 'Rewrote corporate brochure, resulting in a 12 per cent increase in enquiries'.
- Choose a professional font, such as Arial, Verdana, Calibri, or Times New Roman, so a recruiter can scan and read your CV easily. These are readable not only by hiring managers but also by Applicant Tracking Systems (see page 62). Comic Sans is not your friend.

- Present your information in a logical order. Use spacing and section headings, such as 'Work History' and 'Education', to keep things clear.
- Play to your strengths. If you feel a lack of experience is holding you back, lead with education instead. As long as you can relate it back to the role in question, how you order the sections is up to you.

CV-writing don'ts

- Don't be afraid of white space. Even if you think your CV looks a bit bare, as long as you've included all the relevant information and applicable, quantifiable achievements, you needn't worry. Sometimes less is more.
- Don't include your whole work history. The ideal CV should be a checklist of your key accomplishments, not your autobiography. Ask this question before you write anything: 'Will it help me get the job?' If the answer is no, leave it out.
- Don't use too small a font size, or eliminate your margins, in a desperate attempt to cram more into two pages. You're not fooling anyone, and the recruiter will give up in despair if they need to pull out a magnifying glass to read it. A size of 10 or 12 is ideal.
- This should go without saying, but just in case you're one of the crazy ones: don't choose wacky colours, unusual or cursive fonts, or random images.

'I need to see consistency. If you've got one job title in italics and the next one in bold, it just tells me you have no consistency in your approach and no attention to detail.'

Now you've got a feel for what it means to be a CV-writing pro, pull out your lists of jobs, qualifications, and skills that you collected from the last chapter. You'll also need to have the format you've decided on to hand. You're about to put it all together into a dynamite CV.

HOW TO PRESENT YOUR WORK HISTORY

Clearly, the order in which you put your jobs, qualifications, and skills will depend on what format of CV you choose. We're assuming a reverse-chronological format here because that's the most commonly used, but you can adapt these tips to your own needs.

List your jobs from the most recent to the most distant, along with the month and year you began and finished each one, using a consistent heading format. Underneath, add three or four bullet points that cover your key achievements and responsibilities. More recent or relevant jobs may need more bullets, and the opposite is true for ones that are less so. Your task is to highlight what's most likely to get you an interview – in other words, what makes you the best fit for the job.

> *'Nobody gets into sales because they're brilliant with the written word. They do so because they have great people skills. As a result, they're usually highly networked and well known in their vertical market – often they can be 20 years into their careers without ever having to have had to send out a CV. They can usually ace an interview once they get one, but the CV will usually be the one aspect of their application that requires the most TLC.'*

An area that might hold you back is if your current job title doesn't do justice to your level of responsibility, or the nature of what you do. What should you do? Change your job title or embellish your role? Please, no. There are some easy ways around this problem. First of all, clarify your position. If you've been an assistant manager for three years, but have been doing a manager's role for the past year and can pretty much run the place blindfolded, instead of putting 'Assistant Manager' as your job title, put 'Name of company: three years'. Then, clarify in the first bullet point below that you've been working at manager level, but you've never had an updated job title. Whatever you do, don't lie and say you have the title of manager – one fact-checking call from their HR department will blow your cover sky high.

Another common problem is what to do if you've held more than one role at a company. You don't want to hide a promotion or a broadening of your experience. If the jobs were similar in nature, write the company name and list the job titles underneath, like this:

X Company
Personal Assistant (September 2015–Present)
Executive Assistant (January 2013–September 2015)

- Key achievement or responsibility 1
- Key achievement or responsibility 2
- Key achievement or responsibility 3

These bullets should focus on your most impressive accomplishments in both roles combined. If the jobs were in different areas or required very different skills, however, list the company once but break out the titles and treat them as two completely separate roles:

X Company
Personal Assistant (September 2015–Present)

- Key achievement or responsibility 1
- Key achievement or responsibility 2
- Key achievement or responsibility 3

Accounts Co-ordinator (January 2013–September 2015)

- Key achievement or responsibility 1
- Key achievement or responsibility 2
- Key achievement or responsibility 3

HOW TO PRESENT YOUR WORK-RELATED QUALIFICATIONS AND TRAINING

This is an area many recruiters will zoom in on, especially if they've got a requirement for a specific type of training or qualification. If you have a professional qualification that's relevant to the job, make sure that you include it at the beginning of your CV. There's nothing more frustrating for a recruiter than having to check that a candidate for an accountancy role, for instance, has the required qualifications. And if you've taken on training to improve your skills, make sure you list the courses and results. Even if it was something that didn't result in an official qualification, it could still be relevant.

'I need to see if you're qualified for the job first. I hire teachers, and sometimes I'm reading a CV and thinking, "Are they even qualified?" Then I get to the bottom and see they've got a PGCE, but this is something they should be boasting about at the beginning.'

HOW TO PRESENT YOUR SKILLS

It's good to have a separate section for your skills, so a hiring manager can have an immediate sense of what you're good at. There's usually no need to break them down into hard, soft, or transferable skills, unless the specific job you're applying for demands it. The most important thing is to present them in priority order, and with evidence.

You want to end up with around three or four skills listed as bullet points. Make use of your power words, and if you have a long list of them this is where subheadings come in. Group them into categories and name them appropriately. For instance, if you're a teacher who also coaches a football team, label your sections 'Teaching skills' and 'Coaching skills'. Start each category on a new line with the subheading in bold.

HOW TO PRESENT YOUR EDUCATION

By this stage you're probably breathing a sigh of relief. Education should be easy, right? For many people it is, but others might need to tailor their education to their situation.

If you've just left school, list your GCSEs, A levels, and any accomplishments while you were there. Most school-leaver roles won't require much work history, so this is a great way to sell yourself. List the subjects you studied, but feel free to condense them into less-detailed descriptions if you're not sure they're your strongest selling point. And make sure you include things like positions of responsibility (were you a prefect? Did you captain the netball team?) and special achievements.

If you've just left university or college, focus on your degree or highest-level qualification and include school-level information with less detail. Including individual modules isn't necessary but could increase your chances if they relate to the role you're applying for – this is a good way to demonstrate your skills and ability to do the job if you don't have a lot of work history.

If you're still studying, or if you're developing your knowledge by taking an additional qualification, information about your current area of study is likely to be the most relevant. Include any predicted grades and completion dates and expand on the modules you've covered so far if they're directly related to the role.

If it was a long time ago that you left school or university, be brief with your educational qualifications. You only need to include the most recent and high-level one, plus any other work-related certifications you've picked up along the way. A recruiter for a senior management position isn't interested in knowing your GCSE subjects, even if you're particularly proud of your A in Woodwork.

And finally, there's no such thing as the 'school of life'. If you don't have much to show for your education, don't try to hide it or make a joke about it – focus on your areas of strength instead. You'll find out more about this in Chapter 6.

YOUR PERSONAL STATEMENT

Finally we come to the big one. Nothing strikes fear into the heart of a CV writer more than the crafting of the personal statement – it can feel like it's your soul laid bare on the page. What's more, many recruiters advise candidates not to include one at all because they get fed up with dime-a-dozen statements that sound like clones of one another. That doesn't mean, however, that they don't appreciate one, just that a bad statement is worse than none at all. So if you find it hard to write in fluent sentences, use bullets instead. Really, this is worth getting right. And remember, from an employer's perspective a job is a problem to be solved. Your personal statement is the part of your CV that shows them, in a nutshell, why it's you they should be interviewing. No pressure, then.

But first of all, what's a personal statement anyway? From your point of view, it's a paragraph (or a short list of bullet points) which sells you to the recruiter. Not only will you be summarising your skills and experience in it, you'll also be making sure these are relevant to the job you're applying for. But that's not good enough – it also needs to stand out so that your CV passes the seven-second test. Given it's usually at the top of your CV, it's the element that can make or break your application.

'We've seen some candidates expand their personal statement into an achievements section. They have objectives, but also the proof to back them up.'

How to write a personal statement

Once again you find yourself facing the blinking cursor on a blank page. The best solution is to grab a pen and paper – this will take you away from the unnerving blank screen, and somehow, jotting things down freehand allows your creative juices to flow more freely. How to summarise who you are, what you're about, and what makes you special, all in three or four sentences?

1. Start by answering the question: 'Who are you?' Give the hiring manager a powerful statement about who you are and what you do, and include your core values.
2. Next, answer the question: 'What can you offer?' If you're struggling for inspiration, try using the job description to help you to identify the specific skills the employer is looking for. If it shows that they're after someone with excellent business analysis skills, your statement might include: 'Working experience of strategic business analysis, with an investigative and methodical approach to problem solving'.
3. Finally, answer the question: 'What are your career goals?' Remember, you're writing this from the recruiter's perspective – he or she doesn't care what you want to achieve for yourself in five years' time, but about how your plans fit into their company. So craft your goals from the standpoint of what you can offer to them.

'A lot of people use words in their personal statement that don't mean a lot, like "I'm personable, enthusiastic". Think of your CV as being like the image for the Netflix series you choose for the weekend. If it's generic and you're saying the same as everyone else, it's not going to make me want to pick you.'

It's a summary, so keep it concise and to the point. Ideally your statement will be no more than 150 words – any more than this and you'll run the risk of rambling, thereby losing the reader's attention and taking up valuable space. You're best writing it in the present tense, apart from when you're referring to events in the past. This makes it more immediate and personal.

Still having problems?

Are you struggling for inspiration? You're not alone, so try answering this quiz. You may find it easier if a friend asks you the questions and writes down your answers for you, or if you speak into a voice-recording app on your phone. That way you'll be 'in the moment' with your ideas rather than worrying about scribbling them down.

- What made you stand out at school?
- What would your mum say is your best quality?
- What's the job you loved most and why?
- Given a free weekend, what would you choose to do?
- Why do you want this job?
- What do your colleagues say about you?
- What's the achievement you feel most proud of in your work?
- What's the best praise your boss ever gave you?

These are simply aids to start your ideas flowing and to give your confidence a boost, not a template for your answers. Now you're ready to write it for real, but before you do, consider these personal statement dos and don'ts.

Personal statement dos

- Get straight to the point.
- Answer the key questions: who are you? What can you bring to the role? What's your career goal?
- Add value by being specific. Quantify your achievements with numbers, rather than hinting at your success.
- Avoid clichés such as 'team player' and 'goal-oriented'.
- Use the job description to show that you're a perfect fit for the job.
- Employ some of the power words from page 183.

Personal statement don'ts

- Don't be too generic. Tailor your statement to the job instead.
- Don't focus only on yourself. The best personal statements cover the skills you would bring to the company that no other candidate can.
- Don't confuse it with your cover letter or employment history. Your statement is a short introduction, so keep it that way. You need to include concise examples of your career to date, such as 'A financial analyst with eight years' experience', but make them brief.
- Don't think of it as a list, and ensure it's pleasant and varied to read. This means avoiding statements like: 'I am a recent Business Economics graduate. Excellent analytical and organisational skills. I am a driven and self-motivated individual who always gives 100 per cent in everything I do. Proven track record of success'.

'The first thing I want to see are your key achievements. Achievements that are relevant and tangible: "I created technology x, that achieved y and z for the business."'

CHECK, CHECK, CHECK

Your CV is done! Well ... not quite. Before you put the kettle on and click 'send', you need to check it doesn't have any spelling or grammatical mistakes. For this you need a fresh pair of eyes, because when you're checking it's human nature to read what you think is there rather than what you've actually written. Ask an eagle-eyed friend to scan it thoroughly for you, and if you can, make it two friends. Even professional writers have a proof-reader for their work; if you think J.K. Rowling wrote the *Harry Potter* series without editing and proofreading support, you'd be mistaken.

Here are a couple of tips for proofreading: temporarily change the font or read your CV backwards. That way you fool your brain into thinking it's the first time you've read it, and you're more likely to catch your errors. Printing it out is also important, as our eyes naturally read more slowly from printed paper than on a screen. And finally, once you've reviewed it, stop tweaking. It's in the minor changes that oversights creep in – you'll end up with mismatched sentences, or even worse, facts that don't add up.

'Spelling mistakes: we see a lot of Sales Mangers.'

Here's a proofreading checklist:

Spelling and grammar. So simple, and yet so easy to mess up. If you've put yourself forward as a detail person on your CV, this is one area you simply can't afford to get wrong. Check you've got full stops consistently applied and in the right places. Microsoft spell and grammar check are your friends here – those red squiggly lines are often there for a reason.
Names. Have you spelled all the names in your CV correctly?
Tenses. When we speak, we mix our tenses. But when we write, we need to be consistent. Make sure you're using the past tense to

describe your previous experience, and the present to describe what you're doing now.

Sentence length. Be careful not to have run-on sentences that are too long. If you're in doubt, keep them on the short side.

Structure. Look at your CV as a whole. Have you put all your job titles in the same heading format, for instance? There's nothing worse than one heading in italics and the next in bold – it's confusing and gives a poor impression. You want your CV to be easy to skim. For this reason, try not to use more than two formatting styles, such as bold, italics, underline, and font size.

Numbers. One to ten goes in letters, with anything after that in numerals. So it's 'Managed a team of three staff', and 'have 12 years' experience'.

Is it a good read? Does anything sound obscure or deathly dull? Is it logical? Read your CV out loud, because if you stumble on a clumsy sentence the recruiter will too (even though they'll be reading it silently – they're clever like that).

'Someone once separated their CV into four sections.
These were:
Profile
Education history
Work history
Jennifer Aniston'

DOES YOUR CV PASS
THE SEVEN-SECOND TEST?

Finally, you've written your CV and polished it to perfection. But here's the killer question: will it grab the attention of a recruiter? As you know by now, seven seconds is all you get.

> *'All of my clients do their candidate searches in the morning on their commute, and they'll see the top quarter of a CV in their phone preview window. That's how everyone views CVs now.'*

Find out with this checklist:

- Remember the 'Fatal Five' mistakes: a lack of relevant work history, spelling mistakes, frequent job changes, not enough information, and poor visual layout. Have you done something to address all five?
- Does your personal statement focus on who you are, what you can offer, and what your career goals are? Does it relate to the job description? Does it emphasise your most impressive, interesting, and relevant skills and achievements?
- Does your superpower jump off the page? Whether it's having your own blog, taking part in volunteer work, or using social media to network with others in your field, you need something that's relevant to the job to stand out. Present yourself as 'Super You', the person you are on your best day.
- Is the best stuff up front? While you don't want to make your formatting unwieldy, you do need to make sure that the facts you most want a recruiter to read are at the beginning. Think about the position you're applying for: what are your most relevant skills, experiences, and achievements? Don't be afraid to re-jig your template so as to wave all of these strengths in the recruiter's face.
- Have you backed up what you claim to be good at? Use the STAR model to do this: Situation, Task, Action, Result. Summarise the challenge you rose to along with its context, what you did, and the result. For instance, instead of saying you've 'worked on social media', swap this for 'increased social media engagement by 20 per cent through the implementation of a new digital marketing strategy'.

- Is your CV easy and logical to navigate and read? Is it clear and concise? If it takes longer than seven seconds for the reader to scan the most vital points, it's toast.

- Is it no longer than two pages? Only include what is necessary, and don't ramble.

- Are you guilty of using clichés? Phrases like 'excellent team player' and 'goal-driven' will send the recruiter to sleep. You can't bore someone into offering you an interview, so replace those kinds of words with examples of when you've shown you're a great team person instead.

- And finally, have you tailored your CV to the job you're applying for? If not, the next chapter is for you ...

CHAPTER 4

The Fine Art of Tailoring

If you've managed to sort out the basics of your CV by now, you have a right to feel a little smug. It's no mean feat gathering all the information you need, arranging it in a logical order, and presenting it so it grabs a recruiter's attention. But there's more. Maybe you've heard people talking about how you should tailor your CV each time you apply for a job, rather than simply sending out the same one. This is where this chapter comes in.

'Don't be afraid of having more than one CV.'

'What? After all that work, you want me to rewrite my CV for every job I apply for? You have to be kidding.' I get it, it's natural to question putting yet more effort into your CV – after all, you have a life to lead outside of the job-hunting circus. The first objection is that it takes more time. It's true, it does, but consider this: it's far more productive to put an extra hour or two into sending out three CVs that win you an interview than into ten that go straight to the delete folder. The second objection to tailoring is that if you churn out identical CVs you can send your application straight away and beat the competition. A high five to you for wanting to be quick off the mark, but a job hunt isn't a race. No recruiter puts the job advert out, sits waiting by their inbox, and then swoops on the first CV to arrive saying, 'Great! They were quick. Let's give them an interview whatever they're like.' In fact the opposite can be true: many say the first CVs to arrive are often the poorest because they're rushed. The deadline for applications is there for a reason: to give everyone the chance to apply in a certain time frame so that the company can take a look at CVs in one go, or at least in a few batches.

So look on the positive side, because you're about to learn why tailoring is important. You'll also discover how to do it in the quickest and easiest way possible while still achieving excellent results. The reality is, you don't have to write an entirely fresh CV each time, you only need to tweak it. When you know what bits to adjust and how, it's not as hard as it sounds because there is a system.

First, do you need a tailored CV every time?

THE ADVANTAGES

- The big one: you're more likely to be invited to an interview. In my crowdsourced research with recruiting companies, the number one reason for a CV being accepted or rejected was the presence or absence of relevant work history. That means you're more likely to succeed if you can present your work history so it links directly to the job you're applying for. In fact, in my research with recruiters themselves, 80 per cent said candidates should always tailor their CVs.
- When a recruiter sees a CV that instantly connects to the job on offer, it's so much easier for them to say 'I'd like to see that person' than if they have to work out for themselves whether you'd be a good candidate for that particular role.
- It's easier for you to shine in an interview. Interviewers use your CV to give them a steer on what questions to ask, so when your CV is geared to a specific job they'll be questioning you about the areas you want them to focus on.

THE CONSIDERATIONS

- It's a little more work to tailor a CV.
- It depends on how you're applying. For instance, if you're at a conference or event with a few copies of your CV to hand out if opportunity strikes, it's impossible to tailor it.
- Some recruiters think that for people in the later stages of their career a tailored CV isn't necessary, as you're more likely to have built up experience in the sector you're applying to.
- If you have too many versions of your CV it can be confusing when you do the interview (which one did you send?).

'The problem with having too many versions of a CV is sometimes people come in for an interview and you can see they're nervous, struggling to remember which version I'm reading.'

The general advice you'll hear from all recruiters, though, is that tailoring is usually best. Sorry, that's just the way it is. Imagine you were one of them: given the choice between wearing a bespoke outfit lovingly crafted by a master tailor, or an off-the-peg number from your local chain store, which would you go for? The former, of course. The person looking at your CV wants to know that you're a plausible fit for the role, and that you're passionate about fulfilling it well. What's more, they're tired of wading through mounds of CVs that make their life hard by being generic; you stand a much better chance of landing an interview if you join the dots between you and the job for them. Don't be afraid to modify your wording for each job you apply for, altering key terms and swapping your bullet points around. After all, your CV isn't carved in stone, it's a living document that should change according to the role and company you're targeting.

HOW TO TAILOR YOUR CV

From an employer's perspective, a situation has arisen in their organisation that means that a bundle of tasks and responsibilities must be taken up by someone. That special person must have the right mix of skills and talents to fill the role, together with an adaptable, trustworthy, and tenacious mindset. This is the bedrock of tailoring your CV: you need to show how you can do *that particular job* better than anyone else who applies for it.

Let's look first at which CV elements to tailor (good news – you don't always need to do them all). They are your:

- Personal statement
- Work history
- Skills
- Work-related qualifications and training

What's more, tailoring is a pretty simple, two-step process:

1. Research the company and the job, so you know exactly what they're looking for in a candidate
2. Adapt your CV to show why you're the right fit for the specific role on offer

That's it! Are you feeling less daunted now?

> *'I advise applicants to tailor their CVs based on the job specification, pulling out their skills to match what's being asked for. A lot of people apply for jobs in the same sector anyway, so once they've got the tailoring in place they can arrange and rearrange and it's not a big job.'*

SLEUTHING MADE SIMPLE

You know how in the TV detective dramas, the Chief Inspector spends weeks desperately searching for the answer to a mystery murder, only to find that it was staring him in the face all along? Clues to what your recruiter is looking for in a CV are all around you, but to spot them you need to open your eyes and keep a clear head. Let's start first with what you can find out about the company or organisation you're applying to. Where could you look and what will you be seeking to discover?

You'll not be surprised to learn that the internet is your friend here. Check out the company's website and take the time to read a few blog posts if it has any. Look at its values, which you'll usually find in its vision, mission, and CEO statements. What are the organisation's stated goals and purpose? How does it see itself contributing to the world? A company's social media updates can sometimes give you a more up-to-date and realistic picture of what it's like. What's the tone? Is it informal, friendly, stuffy, or even grandiose? Make a note of any key words and phrases that crop up again and again. Now you can start digging deeper, by seeing if they have any press releases or news articles online. You can often find these on the 'Press' tab, or in an area of the website dedicated to relations with investors and the media. These tell you what the company's 'hot spots' are: their current projects and new product releases.

Next, ask around. Who do you know who works there? How about friends of friends? If you're stuck, social media platforms like Facebook and LinkedIn are great for finding out where people are employed (although you'll want to be mindful of privacy if you're keeping your job search secret). You can also take a squint at feedback by their staff on Glassdoor. Gleaning the inside track about the company from real people is a great help when tailoring your CV, and is also useful material for your interview.

PICKING APART THE JOB DESCRIPTION

Take a look at the job advert, and also the full job description if you have one (if not, call the company's HR department and ask if it's available – it often is). Give them a proper read, highlighting the words and phrases that seem important. You'll want to concentrate on the job factors that are mentioned more than once, or that stand out to you. What skills and experience are they after? What does the job entail? Put these in your list.

Now you know a bit about what the company's like and have an understanding of how it sees the role, you're ten steps ahead of the other applicants already. But that's not enough because you'll still be one of many, so here's where you put your new-found knowledge to work. Read your CV and decide what single specific skill or experience is most relevant to this particular job and company – it might be your current position, a qualification you have, or a special project you've completed. Next, find a way of moving it to the top of your CV, creating a new section for it if necessary. Be creative with this. If the key skills in demand are analytical problem solving and experience with spreadsheets, create a section at the top called 'Analytical problem solving and spreadsheet experience'. You've made the recruiter's day that bit easier because you've shown them how you match up to the job, and on the 'yes' pile you'll be more likely to go.

So you've positioned the best bit at the top, where it's clearly visible. What do you do with the rest? You give a new emphasis to the relevant areas of your CV by the way you word them. For instance, if you currently work as a computer programmer and the job description says the ability to work in a team is important, add the fact that you work as part of a team of programmers into your role description. You could even highlight an achievement that you made as part of that team, and why the teamwork was important, rather than only mentioning your solo triumphs.

> *'You can tailor your CV without lying or exaggerating; you just make certain parts stand out so the person who's reading it sees that bit first.'*

Here's a matching exercise to make it easier for you. Take a piece of paper, and on the left-hand side list the skills and experience you've identified as key from the job advert or description you're interested in. On the right-hand side, list your own skills and experience, including soft, hard, and transferable skills. Focus on the top five, so it looks like this:

Job requirements

1. _____
2. _____
3. _____
4. _____
5. _____

My skills and experience

1. _____
2. _____
3. _____
4. _____
5. _____

Now draw a line from each job requirement to one or more of your own skills and experience. You'll notice some of the latter have more than one line ending up at them, and others none at all. The ones with lots of lines are the ones you want to highlight on your tailored CV. Here's an example of a person who's currently a salesperson in a clothing chain store, applying for a job as a sales trainer in an electronics retailer:

Job requirements	My skills and experience
1. Communication skills	1. Five years' experience in sales
2. Understanding of sales process	2. Great at developing a quick rapport
3. Knowledge of electronics	3. Energetic and enthusiastic
4. PowerPoint skills	4. Understands the fashion business
5. Self-motivational attitude	5. Self-reliant

Guess which skills and experience will go at the top of their CV? It'll be sales experience and the ability to develop a rapport with people quickly and easily. The ability to motivate themselves could also go in there as a subsidiary quality. The other job requirements are those they can't demonstrate so easily, but these skills can be learned, so they could emphasise their willingness to develop knowledge about new areas elsewhere in their CV.

THE FUNDAMENTALS OF TAILORING

So you understand the principles behind tailoring your CV, but how do you do it without looking like you're parroting the job advert? You use the relevant skills and experience you picked out above to prove it. Here are some examples of how you can do this.

They want someone who's 'innovative'. Everyone's come up with something new and different at some point or other, so think broadly around this. It might be in any area of your work, or even your private life, that you've dreamed up with a new idea, and you don't have to have been the one who implemented it. It's the innovative outlook they're after. For instance:

- Came up with a new way of storing stock in the warehouse so everyone could reach things more easily

- Increased sales by 6 per cent when I reorganised the store layout more efficiently
- Suggested a new team structure to manager, which reduced staff turnover
- Key words to use: idea, came up with, suggested, innovated, created

They want a 'self-starter'. Highlight the times you've motivated yourself to achieve something of value without being asked, or when you've worked well on your own. Make it clear that you don't need to be managed on a daily basis, and that you enjoy setting yourself challenges rather than having them set for you. For instance:

- Set up a system to alert customers when new stock arrived
- Created a marketing plan for a product launch without being asked
- Offered to contribute to the organisational newsletter
- Key words to use: volunteered, anticipated, independent, unaided, contributed

They want a 'team player'. Point out the occasions when you've worked well with other people to achieve a worthwhile result. For instance:

- Worked with IT department to create voucher scanning system which increased sales by 12 per cent
- Teamed up with colleagues to organise first departmental social
- Collaborated with finance team to set budgets for the next year
- Key words to use: joined, collaborated, worked with, participated, contributed

They want a 'leader'. You don't have to have been in a senior position to have demonstrated leadership skills, but you do need

59

to prove you've given instructions, inspired people, or taught others something new. For instance:

- Inducted two new assistants into the department
- Led a hiking team up a mountain in the company charity walk, inspiring them to carry on in rain and snow
- Managed a team of three, keeping them motivated during a period of cost-cutting measures
- Key words to use: managed, led, supervised, taught, advised, mentored, inspired, influenced, motivated

They want someone who 'loves working with the public'. This is your chance to show how good you are at handling people from outside your organisation, whether it be in a sales role or some other way (you might have been a steward at an event, for example). For instance:

- Handled customer complaints on a helpline for two years, resolving difficulties or passing them to a supervisor as necessary
- Voted 'waiter of the month' five times during a two-year stint at a national restaurant chain
- Managed a department at a department store, combining selling to customers with running the shop-floor team
- Key words to use: served, resolved, facilitated, impressed, handled, supported, provided

'My CV is six pages, but I'd never send that to an employer. I've had two careers (one in IT and one in education) so if I was applying for a job in IT I'd remove the details of my jobs in education but leave the basics on there so there are no gaps. And all of my IT elements I'd put in my key skills.'

Are you seeing how it works? You pick out what they're looking for and show how you've already demonstrated it in your work so far. And in case you're wondering, there's nothing dishonest about this. You're not making anything up or distorting it out of proportion. You're simply shining a light on the areas you want the recruiter to look at while minimising the ones you'd rather they didn't dwell on. It's nothing we wouldn't all do on a first date, is it?

THE POWER OF WORDS

We've touched on specific words and phrases in passing so far, but it's time to look at them in more detail. You'll have picked up by now that it's not just the facts of the job that you need to look at, but the words the company chooses to describe it.

When you mirror the most important words a recruiter uses to outline the role in your CV, the person reading it will have two simultaneous reactions. One is conscious ('She can obviously do the job') and the other subconscious ('There's something about this person I trust'). Your choice of words has a powerful effect. Advertisers discovered this years ago – if we're looking online for a family holiday, we'll seek out words from the travel companies like 'fun', 'beaches', and 'safe'. We may not realise we're doing it, but we do. So if the recruiter's written a job advert using certain words to describe the role and the qualities of the person they're after, those are the words they want to see in your CV even if they're not aware of it. Use them. Trust me, it works.

THE ROBOT FACTOR

There's another implication for your choice of words, which you probably haven't thought of yet, especially if you haven't applied for a job in a few years. It's how to make your CV friendly to an

Applicant Tracking System (ATS). Like it (and believe it) or not, the first scan of your CV may not be by human eyes, but by a computer programme. This isn't the case for every recruiter, but with many jobs receiving hundreds of applications, it's become a necessity for some companies to sort the wheat from the chaff in an automated way. You might feel somewhat affronted by this: 'My painstakingly crafted CV being accepted or rejected by a piece of software!' But it's best to come to terms with this reality and see these systems as your friends rather than your enemies. When you know how to tailor your CV to work with them, your application stands a much better chance of success.

Most recruiters are well versed in ATS software and know how to use it to search for the best candidates. They use what are called Boolean searches to do this. For instance, if they want to find a marketing assistant with an English Literature degree, they search for 'marketing AND assistant AND English Literature AND degree'. If you've included these elements in your CV, you're ticking all the right boxes and will appear at the top of the search results. If you have some of them but not others, you're likely to appear lower in the search results, but you won't necessarily be missed off the list completely. It's just like when you use a search engine to find a website.

So how do these systems operate? There are many types of ATS out there, and they work in slightly different ways, but their primary functions are to:

- Extract and reorganise the various parts of your CV into a common format, so that a human recruiter can compare it more easily with others
- Allow recruiters to search your CV for key words showing how suited to the job you are
- Store and categorise your CV for future reference, in case the company wants to offer you an interview for a different role in the future

- Filter your CV by things like qualifications, location, and previous jobs
- Manage the process so the recruiter can keep track of who's been offered an interview, who's been accepted, and so on

It doesn't look so unreasonable now, does it? You can see why recruiters are working with these systems more and more – they're simply using technology to make their life less complicated. Your main focus as an applicant is to put yourself in a recruiter's shoes so that you can tailor your CV to what they're looking for. Tweaking it in order to go down well with an ATS is part of that process.

HOW TO MAKE YOUR CV ATS-FRIENDLY

How do you ensure that you don't end up in a situation where 'the computer says no'? First of all, it's worth being aware that the ATS is only the first scan of your CV. Once it's passed that level, a human will assess it before deciding whether or not to offer you an interview. So although being ATS-friendly involves jumping over that first hurdle, you want to do it in such a way that when the recruiter does see your CV, they're just as impressed as the computer was. You still need to join the dots for them between 'this is what we're looking for' and 'this is what I will deliver for you when I start work'.

Key words are key. Here's where the key words you identified from your research come into their own. Make sure the key words from the job advert are replicated in your CV so the ATS can easily match your skills and experience to the job. Bear in mind that, depending on the system, the spelling, tense, and singular or plural of the word will be important. So if a hiring manager searches the system for 'computer literate' (because that's what's on the job advert) and you've written 'computer literacy', you may appear lower down their search results. It's the same if they search for '2 years' experience' and you've written 'two', or 'social media experience' and you've written 'Twitter'. You'll still show up, but not as highly as someone who'd used the exact phrases they plugged in. Also, be careful with acronyms – a computer doesn't necessarily know a BA is the same as a degree, for instance, so it's best to write both.

> *'If they've got spelling mistakes they might get missed by an ATS. We might be looking for certain key words or qualifications, and you might have them, but if you haven't put them on your CV you could get overlooked.'*

Frequency of key words can also have an impact, with significant words mentioned more than once bumping you up the list. This is good if you have a genuine reason to repeat them, but tread carefully if not. If you fancy yourself as a bit of a techie, you may have the clever idea of 'stuffing' key words into your CV in white type or ultra-small font to game the system. Or crowbarring a different skill into every sentence – in fact we found one applicant had done this, so he came up in every single employer candidate search no matter what the job was (needless to say, he wasn't offered an interview). Be warned, the system will uncover this and will show you up at the same time. It's best not to bother.

Focus on your hard skills. Another robot-like feature of an ATS is that it prefers hard to soft skills. Commonly used soft-skill phrases like 'team player' and 'hard working' aren't quantifiable, so recruiters don't tend to search for them. That doesn't mean you shouldn't put soft skills on your CV, but that you should make extra sure you've included and worded your hard skills in the right way. These include your qualifications, job titles, and experience in areas relevant to the job, because those are the key words they'll be checking for.

Use the right format. An ATS finds it hard to read PDFs and prefers Word file formats (so do 73 per cent of human recruiters, in fact). It also doesn't like clever graphics and images as, being a robot, it has an undeveloped sense of style. Don't try to impress it with the fancy stuff.

Crafting your CV so it's ATS-friendly involves balancing the demands of the computer and the person, but it's totally achievable. You want to include the right words in the right way for the ATS, but at the same time ensure that when it reaches a human it still makes a strong impression. What's more, in the process of doing this you'll be giving a laser focus to how you present yourself on your CV, which is no bad thing in itself.

> *'Some of the jobs that we work on have different job titles that could be applied to them, but we would know to search for the variants.'*

You'll be pleased to know that you've taken writing your CV as far as it can go now. In the next chapter you'll learn how to tackle that most tricky of tasks: creating the perfect cover letter.

CHAPTER 5

Craft the Perfect Cover Letter

If your CV is the golden arrow that lands you the interview, your cover letter is the bow that shoots it. It's one more chance to show why you're right for the job, and to let your personality shine through. It's also the element that can feel most tedious. You've lovingly written and polished your CV. Surely that's enough? Why the need for a cover letter to go with it? And aren't they a bit old fashioned nowadays, in any case? The short answer is: for the majority of jobs you need one, so read on to find out how yours can make or break your application.

First of all, what's a cover letter for? A cover letter is an introduction to your CV, setting the scene and encouraging the recruiter to look at your CV in a positive light. When it comes to crafting your cover letter, you can see it as a blessing or a curse. On the one hand it's a relief not to be restricted by those CV bullet points (along with the dreaded key words), but at the same time the freedom of a letter format can send you off piste into dangerous territory. This can make filling the page daunting, especially if you don't rate your writing skills too highly. But once you understand what your cover letter is for and how it differs from your CV, it becomes a simpler task, especially when you realise there's a process to follow.

> *'If you're going to submit a cover letter it has to be bespoke and talk about why you're applying for the job. It's a great opportunity to talk about your mindset, which isn't always easy on a CV. If it's generic, don't bother.'*

If there's one thing to remember, it's this: don't be boring. The seven-second rule applies to your cover letter as well as your CV. This is a golden place to take a calculated risk in order to stand out.

HOW TO WRITE YOUR COVER LETTER

Here's the process for creating a cover letter that will do your CV proud. Follow these five steps and you can't go far wrong.

1. Research the role and the company so you can make your cover letter specific and relevant
2. Find out who to address it to
3. Structure and write it
4. Format it
5. Send it

That's it! Here's what to do in each step.

1. Research the role and the company

The one thing that will send your cover letter winging its way into the recycle bin is if it doesn't show – in seven seconds – why you're worth having in for an interview. And as you know by now, that means convincing the recruiter you're better qualified for that particular job than any other applicant. To do this you need to find out what the company does, who its competitors are, who they sell to, what the job involves, and the essential skills and experience they're after. Please don't skip this step. Demonstrating that you understand the company core values tells a hiring manager that you have an interest in joining their company, not just any company.

2. Find out who to address it to

Many companies' internal mail systems are labyrinths; what goes in rarely finds its way out. So sending your cover letter and CV to 'The Hiring Manager' or 'Head of Recruitment' is a great way of making sure it's never seen again. It sounds obvious, but address it to the person dealing with the applications. This should be on the job advert, but if not don't be afraid to find out by visiting the company's website or simply calling them up. Not only will you be able to send it to the right person, but you'll also show initiative.

Start with 'Dear Mr Smith/Ms Jones'. If you really can't find a name, use 'Dear Sir/Madam', but this is a last resort. At the very least try to discover the name of the most senior hiring manager and address it to him or her – at least it looks like you've tried.

In terms of the addressing format, put the person's name, company name, company address, and the date at the top left of the letter. Then put your own address at the top right. See our basic cover letter template on page 182, or download a ready-to-use version from https://www.reed.co.uk/career-advice/free-cover-letter-template/

3. Structure and write it

Of course, there's more than one way to write a cover letter, but this is a fail-safe format.

Paragraph one: open the letter

Why are you sending your CV? Be clear and to the point so there's no doubt which job you're applying for. Recruiters also like it if you tell them where you found the advert, and if someone in the organisation referred you, mention their name as it could add credibility.

Do say: 'I wish to apply for the role of IT Manager, currently being advertised on reed.co.uk. Please find attached my CV for your consideration.'

Don't say: 'Please find attached my CV.' It doesn't tell the recruiter anything useful.

Paragraph two: explain why you're suitable for the job

You're moving into selling yourself now. Briefly describe what makes you great for the role, ensuring that you refer to each of the skills listed in the job description.

Do say: 'As you will see from my CV, I have over three years of experience in the IT industry, including 18 months in the retail sector. The knowledge and skills I built up during this time make me an ideal candidate for the role.'

Don't say: 'I'd love to develop my career in IT.' This is all about you, and it doesn't give the recruiter a reason to give you an interview.

Another option here is to make your cover letter more seven-second-friendly by throwing in a memorable fact, showing your passion, or revealing an achievement that makes you stand out. For instance, 'I love proving to people that IT isn't boring by showing them what it can achieve, which is why I developed a stock-tracking system during my lunch breaks in my last company. The sales team loved it.'

Paragraph three: tell them what you can do for the organisation

A job never exists in isolation. It has been created to contribute to the company's success. Outline how your skills and experience are relevant to the position you're applying for, and expand on a couple of points in your CV. Remember to include examples to back up your claims.

Do say: 'In my current role as Senior Programmer at Software Company X, I have been responsible for developing systems which increased client enquiries by 156 per cent in under 12 months. This helped the business increase its revenue by 55 per cent year on year.'

Don't say: 'I'm currently working as a Senior Programmer and have the skills for the job.' It doesn't give the hiring manager anything to go on.

This area is also your chance to show you've done your research and explain how you could benefit this specific company, rather than the industry as a whole. After all, the employer wants to know how you could be an asset to them, not to everyone else.

Do say: 'I've been following Software Company Y for many years now, and your success in website development and scanning software makes you stand out from your competition in the app sector. I believe my skills in app development could help your company develop more of a competitive edge.'

Don't say: 'I think I'd be a great fit for this position at your company and am keen to enter this thriving industry.' Why would a recruiter offer you an interview after reading a generic phrase like that?

Paragraph four: tell them again

Here's where you reiterate your interest in the role and why you would be the right fit for it. It's also the perfect place to indicate that you'd love the chance to be interviewed. 'Finish strong' as they say.

Do say: 'I am confident that I can bring this level of success with me to Software Company Y, and help you build your reputation as one of the UK's fastest-growing software houses. Thank you for your time and consideration, and I look forward to meeting with you to talk about how I might contribute to your future success.'

Don't say: 'I can fit you in for an interview next Tuesday and will be in touch to arrange a time.' No recruiter likes presumption.

Close the letter

Sign off with 'Yours sincerely' (if you know the name of the hiring manager), or 'Yours faithfully' (if you don't), followed by your name.

4. Format it

Your cover letter should be concise and easy to read, so use a professional font such as Arial, Verdana, Calibri, or Times New Roman, and don't get carried away with embellishments. No pictures, Comic Sans, 'handwritten' fonts, and definitely no WordArt. You also want to make sure it's the right length. Too long and you risk rambling and boring the recruiter, too short and you'll sell yourself similarly. Aim for half a side of A4, or certainly no more than one whole side.

5. Send it

If you're posting your cover letter and CV via old-fashioned mail, this is easy – you just put them both in an envelope and you're away. In fact, so few people do this now that it's become an effective way to stand out. A friend of mine even received a couple by hand and ended up hiring both contenders as he knew it took a lot of courage to do that. But now that most CVs are emailed, how to deliver them so that they are read can pose a dilemma. There are three options:

1. Sending both documents as attachments, with a brief explanatory email
2. Sending your CV as an attachment, but copying and pasting your cover letter into the body of your email

3. As per option 2, but adding your cover letter as an attachment along with your CV

When we spoke to recruiters about their preferences around this we found a range of options, so if in doubt, cover all your bases and go for option 3. This minimises the hassle for attachment-haters, but also caters for those who want a professional-looking letter to print out.

> *'Sometimes people will do a cover letter for a CV, but it's a generic one, so they send it to you and it's addressed to the wrong person or it's for the wrong role. It suggests a lack of concentration and effort.'*

COVER LETTER FAQS

Cover letters are one of those areas that people have a lot of questions about. My research with jobseekers threw up plenty, so here are my answers (all gleaned through talking with employers and our recruitment consultants alike).

Do I always need a cover letter? The recruiter didn't ask for one. 92 per cent of recruiters told us that they would consider a CV without a cover letter, so they're clearly not essential in every circumstance. However, you want to be more than considered, you want to be selected, and a well-crafted cover letter can help with that. Also, bear in mind that if you're not asked for one, it might be because the recruiter simply assumed you'd send one. Even if that's not the case, including one without being prompted gives you a good chance of standing apart from those candidates who chose not to make the effort.

What if there are gaps in my work history? Good news – your cover letter is the perfect opportunity to explain them briefly, honestly, and positively. You don't want prospective employers to jump to worrying conclusions about your work ethic. For instance, 'I took a career break to have a family', or, 'I broadened my horizons by volunteering abroad'. On the other hand, bringing personal issues or excuses into the mix is never a good idea, nor is lying.

> *'I recently came across a CV from someone who had experience of working in a "whorehouse". I think they meant "warehouse" ... I hope, anyway.'*

I'm applying to a company speculatively, so can't match my cover letter to a specific job. What do I do? If you're applying for a role that's not advertised, you won't have a job specification to work from. But that doesn't mean you can't tailor your letter. Instead of using an advert as a guide, give a full description of the kind of role you're looking for along with any relevant experience, knowledge, and education that will prove your suitability. A cover letter for a speculative application is also a great platform for showing your knowledge of, and interest in, the company, so use it to express why you want to work there and what you'll bring to the party.

What do I say if I'm not fully qualified for the role? This can make things tricky, but the worst tactic is to draw attention to your shortcomings. Instead, use your cover letter to highlight your most impressive skills and qualifications – the ones that make up for the areas you're lacking in. It's a brilliant chance for you to explain your transferable skills in more detail. For instance, if you're applying to be the manager of a clothing store but have only worked as an accounts manager before, give examples of how your skills could transfer to the new role. It could go something like this:

'I can offer you strong leadership ability: in my current role I led a team of five through a time of business-wide upheaval, with no loss of enthusiasm or productivity. I also have a detail-oriented approach – at my previous company, for instance, I prevented a major loss of profit by discovering a flaw in a colleague's sales projections. And finally, I have a keen interest in fashion. My profitable side-business trading retro clothing on eBay has given me experience in selling direct to customers, and an appreciation of some of the challenges your business faces in doing so.'

Should I bring out my personality? Absolutely! Don't think that because your cover letter isn't about you, but about the company and job you're applying for, that you're not allowed to be yourself. Take advantage of the freedom the letter format gives you to bring out what makes you you. If you're happy describing yourself as 'a whizz with spreadsheets', that's great – as long as you have the personality to match. Your aim is to elevate your letter from the 'blah blah' every recruiter is sick of, to the one that perks them up. A little humour can also work well, if used wisely. Take this example from one we've seen: 'Since the day I collapsed my pushchair by unscrewing the bolts at the age of two, I've been obsessed with how things fit together, which is what makes me so well suited to an engineering role. If I were to work for you, though, I promise I'd leave your office chair alone.'

Should I include salary information in my cover letter? Employers are looking for candidates who can follow directions, so if the advert doesn't mention anything about your current salary you're safest leaving it out. But if they do, give a range instead of exact figures – this will allow you some leeway for negotiation. And if you're asked about your salary expectations and don't want to give anything away yet, it's perfectly acceptable to say they're negotiable.

COVER LETTER MISTAKES

Here are the top mistakes we see at Reed. If all you do is avoid these errors, you'll already be ahead of the pack.

Using the same letter for every job application. This will save you time, but it won't gain you an interview. A mass-manufactured letter is easy to spot. It's stuffed with generic phrases and has a lack of specific information about the company or role you're applying for – clues that make it the work of seconds for a recruiter to sniff out. You might also be including information that isn't even relevant to the job, which shows a lack of interest and diverts attention from the dazzling details you could be revealing.

'I very rarely get a cover letter that's not generic.'

Regurgitating your CV. Your cover letter gives you the chance to expand (in full and fluent sentences) on the bullet points in your CV, so grab the opportunity to highlight your significant achievements and 'greatest hits'.

Making it all about you. As I've said before, a job is a problem that an employer wants to find someone to solve. This means that your application shouldn't be based on what you want, but on what they're seeking. Of course you should talk about your achievements, skills, and experience, but only if they relate directly to the vacancy you're applying for. Avoid detailing your hopes and dreams, and don't explain what you'd personally get out of the job. A cover letter isn't there for you to fulfil your objectives, it's about you proving to a recruiter that you have what it takes to fulfil theirs.

Being overly personal. Maybe you're short of money or have had an unlucky run of job rejections. Life is tough sometimes, but that doesn't make this information cover letter-friendly. It's never okay to talk about your personal life or to share irrelevant facts. Other personal topics, such as the reasons for leaving your current job, overly detailed justifications for career breaks, or how your boss has always had it in for you, fall firmly into the 'do not mention' category.

Drawing attention to your weaknesses. A recruiter isn't interested in what you can't do, they only want to know what you can. If you're lacking in experience in certain areas but have strengths in others, just focus on your strong points. Negativity has no place in a cover letter, so if something doesn't prove why you should be given an interview it's not worth including.

Being too keen. Enthusiasm is great, but desperation is not. Your application on its own tells the recruiter you're interested, so there's no need to go overboard in your cover letter. Begging for the job isn't going to add anything to your selling potential, and if you appear desperate the recruiter will assume that you're not in high demand. That doesn't stop you being enthusiastic, which is certainly a positive, but explain it by saying why you think the organisation would be great to work for and mention some of their successes while you're about it.

Trying too hard. A hopeful accountant sent a cover letter to the Reed accounts department in response to a job we advertised. In it he listed his 'lifetime achievements', which included saving a child from 'possible death' during an attack by wild deer, and attacking and killing a cobra snake. Clearly delighted with his accomplishments, he assured us that this showed he was ready to prove himself and work hard 'for the betterment of the organisation'. Sometimes, sticking to the requirements in the job advert is all it takes (although to be fair, he was certainly memorable).

The old chestnuts: using clichés, not proofreading, underselling or overselling yourself, being arrogant, and lying. All ones to avoid.

> 'All I can say is the candidate was "experienced in shi[f]t work". That quote was used many a time in our office to remind people to proofread!'

You're now ready to send off your CV and cover letter. But what if you're worried about a particular problem in applying for your dream job, such as being inexperienced, or having gaps in your employment history? The next chapter is for you.

CHAPTER 6

CV Challenges

It's one thing to create a CV when the job you're applying for is the natural next step. Doing it when you have a specific challenge to overcome is another. What if you're after a job that you don't have the right experience for? What if you have gaps in your work history, and you're worried that they'll make you look unreliable? What if you're a school or college leaver with no experience? There are a host of reasons why you might feel that the standard CV advice doesn't apply to you.

There's no getting away from the fact that when you have a hurdle to leap over, creating your CV becomes a little more testing. But, as with most problems in life, there's usually a solution. This chapter takes the most common reasons for feeling worried about your application and gives you easy ways to overcome them. When you see how simple it is to resolve your particular issue, you'll also realise that there's no need to stifle your dreams when it comes to applying for a 'problem' role. It all comes down to thinking like a recruiter.

> *'Sometimes people will view CVs on their phone, so you've got to make the recruiter want to scroll down.'*

To help you in your quest to win an interview against the odds, career advice experts at Reed have created a set of CV templates for you. You'll find them on pages 166–80, and you can also download ready-to-use versions at ww.reed.co.uk/career-advice/

cvs/cv-templates. So when I refer to formats and templates, this is where to go. My crowdsourced research with jobseekers revealed that almost 20 per cent had used a template they found online, so don't use just any old template, use one of ours.

> *'Employers like the reverse-chronological*
> *CV format because it shows up*
> *any gaps.'*

These templates are only a starting point and you need to customise them to meet your specific needs. They'll make life easier for you, but there's no need to feel constrained by them – use them wisely and flexibly.

WHAT'S YOUR SITUATION?

Here are the main issues that, in Reed's experience, jobseekers encounter when they're not applying for the most obvious role for them. I'll cover each in turn, so by all means jump to the section that best describes you – even if you can't find the exact fit, there's sure to be advice you can use from at least one of these. What situation best describes you?

- You have no relevant experience
- You're underqualified
- Your work history is full of gaps
- You're a job hopper
- You're overqualified
- You're straight out of school or university
- You think you're too young or too old
- You want a part-time or flexible role
- You're not working at the moment
- You have something to hide

You have no relevant experience

You've been toiling away as an accounts assistant for three years now, and have finally come to the realisation that number crunching isn't for you – instead, you'd love to break into sales. That's okay, we all live and learn. But how do you land that coveted sales job interview when your work history is about as appropriate for it as a fork is for eating soup? You're right to be concerned, and you're not alone. In my research with jobseekers, a lack of relevant work history was assumed to be the number one reason for their CV landing in the reject pile, and the recruiters I asked agreed. There's no getting around the fact that this is an issue, but on the other hand, think of all the people who've succeeded in making a career change. If we all stayed on the same path we started out on after school or university, life would be very dull. TV host Ellen DeGeneres worked as a bartender, waitress, store assistant, house painter, and oyster shucker before she broke into presenting. Actor Harrison Ford temporarily gave up acting in order to gain a steady income as a carpenter before he made his name in *Star Wars*. And singer Elvis Costello was a computer programmer in the early days of IT, before he released his first hit single.

> 'Something that I'd like to see more of in sales CVs is a subsection outlining the type of client you sell to (e.g. oil and gas companies). That way, even if the product you're selling is completely different to that of the company you're applying to, you'd be using transferable skills. Often I think this is even more important than the product being the same.'

You think

I'm so bored with my job and I know this field isn't for me – I just need to break into something I'd be great at. How can I convince a recruiter I'm worth the risk?

The recruiter thinks

Why should I take a chance on this applicant, when there are a hundred others who have relevant experience? They seem like a safer bet.

Your CV strategy

Focus on your transferable skills, and find ways of showing you have what it takes to succeed even if you don't have the direct experience for the role. You're wanting to demonstrate that you have the right mindset.

Top-line tactics

Make sure you fully understand the skills and experience detailed in the job advert. What's required to make a success of the role? These might not be the obvious things. If you can, talk to people already in that field so you can glean the inside track on what their day-to-day work involves. For instance, 'preparing accounts' might mean gathering data from around the company (which could involve being persuasive), arranging it logically, and being meticulous. Can you show you've done these kinds of tasks already?

Next, work out what transferable skills you already have, which would 'prove' you can do the job (you might want to take a look at page 25 again, where there's a handy exercise to help you work them out). While you're doing this, take an objective look at your work history. What were the key tasks and responsibilities in your previous jobs that could relate to the one you're going for? For instance, if you're currently a teacher and want to move into marketing, you've probably developed skills in presenting persuasively, problem solving, and working independently. These are all relevant, but have you also done any marketing-related tasks, such as contributing to the school newsletter, managing its Twitter feed, or applying for funding? What were your results? If a recruiter sees that you've been successful in these, they'll be less concerned about your inappropriate work background.

> *'If you're a sales person and you're applying for another sales person role, you know what is needed in your industry. But if you're applying to a new industry, you need to say why you're looking for that role. If I think of the most successful career switchers, few of them have had relevant experience, but they've been able to demonstrate why they want to change.'*

Once you've identified your transferable skills and experience, think about what CV format you need. My career-change CV template (see page 180) starts with your transferable skills and then goes onto your work history, rather than the other way around. This helps you to show that you understand what's needed in the new role, and how you can fulfil it. You'll also want to craft your personal statement so that it showcases your transferable skills and experience, and explains the main reason for your career shift. It's helpful for a hiring manager to know why you want to change, so they can feel reassured it's been well thought through. You don't want to come across as someone who'll apply for anything just so you can escape your current situation. Try this for inspiration:

Example: 'As an experienced sales manager, my tenacious and proactive approach resulted in numerous important contract wins. My excellent networking skills have provided my team with vital client leads, and my ability to develop client relationships has resulted in a 28 per cent increase in business renewals for my current organisation. After eight years in sales, I am currently seeking a new challenge that will make use of my meticulous attention to detail, and my friendly, professional manner.'

> *'Sometimes we'll get people saying in their*
> *personal profile that they're interested in developing*
> *a career in marketing, but they're applying for*
> *a sales role.'*

As you can see, when it comes to writing your CV and cover letter, don't be apologetic. 'I know I don't have the experience but …' is giving the recruiter an easy reason to bin your application. Instead, talk about your transferable skills and experience, and back them up with evidence of when you've achieved success. You could try something like, 'I changed the format of the school's charity fundraising circular so it was more reader-friendly, which resulted in a 33 per cent increase in donations.'

Finally, be realistic. You have to be reasonably sure you're capable of doing the role you're after, especially if it's in a completely new field. It's not just about what you want, it's ultimately about what you can contribute. You'll probably have to be prepared to start low and work your way up, but that's a small price to pay if it's the industry you dream of.

You're underqualified

Let's face it, when we apply for a new job it's usually because we want a step up. It's rare to meet the jobseeker who says, 'I fancy a demotion this time, that's why I'm lowering my sights and going for a junior role.' So there's nothing unusual, or wrong, about being somewhat underqualified for the job you're applying for. But the key word is 'somewhat'. There's a difference between being almost there, and being woefully unsuitable. Which one are you?

You think

I can do this job standing on my head now, and I'm desperate for a promotion. I've just found a great role, but they're asking for an

English degree/BTech Level 3/five years' experience in a specific area, and I don't have it. What can I do?

The recruiter thinks

Why does this person think they've got a chance when they're obviously underqualified? I'd rather give an interview to someone who can tick the right box.

Your CV strategy

First of all, work out if being underqualified really is a hindrance. For some jobs, especially in a professional or technical field, you'll need a specific qualification before they'll even consider you, so don't waste your time applying for roles you'll never be taken seriously for. But if your research shows that the qualification or experience is more of a 'nice to have' than an 'essential', your task is to show why you not having it shouldn't matter to them. They may say that they're looking for someone with ten years' experience when you have six, but that shouldn't stop you going for it.

Top-line tactics

These are similar to those you'd employ if you didn't have relevant work history (see above). Focus on what you *do* have in the way of qualifications and experience, rather than on what you *don't*. State what you've got and explain why it's gone no further as yet, together with your plans to make up the difference – being motivated to learn is an attractive attitude in a candidate. Sometimes recruiters put a specific requirement into a job advert as a way of reducing the overwhelming number of applications. That doesn't mean that they're never going to be interested in you, but that you'll have to work that bit harder to attract their attention. Recruiters, just like small children, don't always receive everything they put on their Christmas list. They're often willing to sacrifice the odd qualification or year of experience for the person with the desired mindset.

> *'I saw one CV in which the candidate wrote that he was*
> *responsible for the "destruction" at his current employer.*
> *It turned out he was responsible for the distribution.'*

Another tactic is to highlight the advantages of not having the requirements. Instead of spending three years studying for a business degree, maybe you actually set up your own business, or instead of the five years in graphic design they're asking for, maybe you created your own website, designed the logos for your friends' businesses, and trained yourself in image manipulation software. You might also like to take a risk to get your CV noticed – after all, you've nothing to lose. You'll read lots of tips on that in Chapter 8. And finally, be enthusiastic in your cover letter, showing the most positive side of your personality. Giving the impression that you'd be a great person to work with, despite your possible shortcomings, never does any harm.

In terms of what CV format to use, it depends on the area you're underqualified in. If it's in an educational or training qualification, use the basic reverse-chronological template (see page 166), as this has education and training towards the end. If it's work history you lack, try our career-change template (see page 180).

Your work history is full of gaps

Having a CV with more employment gaps than a struggling Hollywood actor is no fun. Unless you're a complete couch potato, they probably weren't by choice. Possibly you've been made redundant a couple of times, relocated because of your partner's job, or went back into education for a while. Even if you chose the gaps, it's likely to be because you were doing other important things – like raising a family, looking after your elderly parents, or travelling the world. Without people like you, the world would be a less interesting and less compassionate place.

*'Employers may be less worried about gaps, but will be
more concerned about whether or not you have the skills
to do the job.'*

This being said, having gaps in your work history can do you a
disservice – for no other reason than recruiters are a suspicious
lot. With hundreds of applications to sort through, they're quick
to find easy reasons to reject people, and a bullet-ridden CV is
one of them. So, how do you work around this problem?

You think

It's so unfair. The gaps in my work history aren't my fault, but
they hold me back. I need a job now more than ever to put my
career back on track. Why won't anyone give me a chance?

The recruiter thinks

This applicant looks a bit suspect. What's with that three-year
break here, and that six-month space there? They might be okay,
but without knowing the facts I'll steer clear.

Your CV strategy

Don't think of your gaps as holes, think of them as other roles
that you didn't happen to be paid for. What did you do during
your time 'off'? What did you learn? What did you achieve?
Focusing on this, rather than the void, is the key.

Top-line tactics

Explain the gaps when you write your CV. Don't cross your fingers
and hope recruiters won't notice – rest assured, they will. When
you're listing your jobs include the gaps, and in your bullet points
explain the reasons for them along with a couple of key achievements if possible. Word them positively, too. 'Gained a BTech in
childcare to improve my qualifications after redundancy' is more
persuasive than, 'Went to evening college after I lost my job'.

Your personal statement also comes into play here. If you're currently unemployed or between jobs, give the reason briefly (don't apologise) and say why you're applying for the role. You can also mention something important you've learned or achieved at the same time – it's all about confidence.

> *'If you've left your job because of a disagreement, leave it off your CV but be honest if you're asked about it.'*

For your CV format recruiters prefer the basic reverse-chronological, so use this if you possibly can (see page 166). Also, if your gaps are pretty minor (covering months rather than years), consider just listing the years rather than the months you started and ended work. However, if your work history shows more time out of work than in, the career-change template (see page 180) is a good one. It starts with your skills and then goes on to your work history, rather than the other way around, which helps you to focus on the positive. You do still need to list your work history along with the gaps, though – don't miss them out.

You're a job hopper

Sometimes it takes a while to work out what you want to do. You land a job in IT, but after a year you decide it's not for you and switch to marketing. Unfortunately, six months is all it takes for you to realise that agonising over logo colours feels like time you're never going to get back, so you jump to sales. After a couple of years on the road your first baby arrives and it becomes impractical, so ... (you can see where this is heading).

It's not unusual to try a few different job types or sectors before you discover what's right for you. But when your career path has more zigzags than a Christmas jumper, you need to see it from a recruiter's viewpoint. You're obviously capable of landing jobs in new areas or you wouldn't have had success so far, but there comes a time when you worry your luck is running out. Maybe this is that time.

'Years ago it was almost looked down upon for someone to have jumps in their CV, with six months here and there, but nowadays it's more acceptable to hop around from job to job.'

You think

It's not my fault I've struggled to find my passion. We should all try new things, and at least I have broad experience. Now I know what I want to do, so how can I put myself across as consistent and trustworthy?

The recruiter thinks

How am I supposed to know what this person is good at? They've done a bit of everything. And what's to say they wouldn't jump ship from this job just like they've done with all the others?

Your CV strategy

Figure out the continuity in your history – there must be a common reason why you shifted from one path to another. Maybe your diversion into teaching from banking was because you enjoyed training new recruits and wanted to take it further. Or possibly your move from the automotive to the fashion sector was because you discovered you were talented at design. Join the dots for the recruiter to show that there's 'method in your madness' and that you have what it takes to stick at your next job.

'If you've got a steady career progression that's fine, but if you've done a lot of contract work, you don't want people to think you're a job hopper so put your reasons for leaving on your CV.'

Top-line tactics

Pick and choose the elements of your work history that are most relevant to the job you're applying for, and highlight those in your bullet points. Think of the story you're telling the recruiter – does it add up? Also, this is not the time to be shy about your achievements. You have to work extra hard to convince them that you can deliver what the job requires, in order to make up for your patchy work history.

Your personal statement is the best place to show the links between the various jobs you've done and why they are relevant for the one you're applying for now. For instance, if it's a computer programming role, you could mention that you were the first of your college friends to develop your own software programme, and how when you were an accountant you created a complex spreadsheet system to help you keep track of the figures. You're showing a long-term enthusiasm for, and ability in, IT. This will help to reassure the recruiter that you're not simply a flaker who gets bored easily, but have just taken a while to realise what you're great at.

For your CV format, the basic reverse-chronological (see page 166) is best – recruiters prefer it because it's honest and open. But you'll want to ensure that you use bullet points that highlight the relevant skills and work history for the specific job you're applying for, and leave out the rest.

You're overqualified

There are times when it's right to go for a job you're overqualified for. It might be because you want to downshift, thereby reducing your responsibilities and stress. Or it could be due to a relocation or the desire to divert to a new industry, and the available jobs are all below your current level – gaining one of those, and making your way back up, seems like the best option. So how do you convince a recruiter to take you seriously? Most of the candidates they'll be looking at will be seeking a move up, not down. And while any hiring manager will be delighted to receive a CV that shows that you can ace the job, they'll also worry that you'll quickly become bored with it ... thereby creating another vacancy for them to fill before they know it.

You think

Why won't anyone give me an interview because I'm too well qualified? It doesn't make sense. Alternatively: I'm so much better qualified than all the other candidates, I'll smash this (not necessarily).

The recruiter thinks

Why on earth is this person applying for the job? They'll end up leaving within six months. It looks a bit suspect to me.

Your CV strategy

Be clear why you're applying for a job you're overqualified for, and show how you've stuck at jobs for decent lengths of time in the past. That way, you'll allay the recruiter's main fears. Whatever you do, don't underplay your qualifications or experience in an attempt to 'fit in' with the rest of the candidates – they're your strongest cards.

Top-line tactics

Showing your enthusiasm for the job in question is vital, so use your personal statement to explain what appeals to you most about it. Also, detail how this position will play to your strengths. For instance, if you're going for a post as a teaching assistant when you're currently a fully qualified teacher, you could say that you love spending time with the kids individually rather than managing the whole classroom. Also, your teaching experience means that you'll understand intuitively how to help your own teacher without being told what to do. Whatever you do, be honest – don't make up reasons which won't stack up at interview.

The basic reverse-chronological CV format (see page 166) is ideal for you, because it showcases your impressive experience and qualifications. Remember, never apologise for being over-qualified, but at the same time be ready to explain it.

You're straight out of school or university

The age-old dilemma of the school leaver or recent graduate never changes: you need experience to make it to your first proper job, but no-one will consider you without experience. In fact, my research with over 2,000 recent graduates showed that on average, they took three to four months to land their first roles. But no matter how frustrating this catch-22 situation can be, you can overcome it if you craft your CV in the right way.

You think

How can I land an interview without experience? It seems like that's all recruiters are interested in.

The recruiter thinks

Why give an interview to a wet-behind-the-ears school or college leaver when there are more experienced candidates lining up for it? They'd have to be pretty special for me to consider them.

Your CV strategy

Note the 'special' element of what recruiters are looking for. Hiring managers are attracted to candidates with the right mindset as much as – if not more than – the right experience, so highlight your soft and transferable skills to give a flavour of the kind of person you are. It may be worth going back to Chapter 2 at this point, for a refresher on unearthing what those skills are.

Here are the skills and qualities that, in my experience, are most prized by graduate employers:

- Creative problem solving
- Commercial awareness
- Adaptability
- Getting on with people
- Time management
- Being confident
- Being self-aware
- Decision-making ability
- Working under pressure
- Initiative
- Emotional intelligence

Top-line tactics

In the absence of much work history, your personal statement comes into its own here. Use it to emphasise your enthusiasm for the job, together with any skills and experience (even if not work related) that show your suitability. Remember, all experience is good experience if you present it in the right way. Also make it clear that you have a plan for where you want to go – hiring managers love to see energy and ambition in a young person. Here are a couple of examples of how you could go about this:

School leaver

Answer the following three questions: Why do you want to work in this industry? What skills make you right for the role (hint: use the job description)? Where do you want to go in your career? Focus especially on the latter, and on what you can bring to the business.

Example: 'A highly motivated and hardworking person, I have recently completed my A-Levels with excellent grades in Maths and Science. I am seeking an apprenticeship in the engineering sector to build upon a keen scientific interest, and to start a career as a maintenance engineer. My eventual career goal is to become a fully qualified and experienced maintenance or electrical engineer, with the longer-term aspiration of moving into project management.'

Graduate

This is similar to the school-leaver example, but paying extra attention to the areas you've studied during higher education. Again, explain why you're applying and where you'd like to go in your career, as well as the specific skills or knowledge you can offer. But also drop in a few more details about your degree.

Example: 'A recent business economics graduate with a 2:1 honours degree from the University of X, I am looking for a graduate analyst role to develop my analytical skills in a practical and fast-paced environment. My goal is to do a job that gives me responsibility for the analysis and interpretation of commercial data, for a well-respected and market-leading company.'

Don't forget to list the work history you do have, even if it only consists of weekend or evening roles. These show that you can hold down a job and know how to deliver for a boss, and they give you the chance to talk about what you've achieved and learned. It's easy to underestimate these, but a bar job shows that you can rub along with people, be trusted with cash, and juggle competing priorities. It's well worth having a bullet point for one main achievement that will make a great impression, too. Did you implement a new project, make an innovative suggestion, or overcome a particular challenge during your work?

> 'A candidate once popped on the end of his CV that if I gave him the job he would make me a cake every week. Sadly he didn't get it.'

You're also in a great position to make use of social media to back up your CV. My research revealed that over a quarter of graduates are on LinkedIn, and over one in five uses Facebook to land their first job. You'll find out more about how to bolster your online presence in relation to your CV in Chapter 8. For your CV format, you can use the school-leaver (page 170) and graduate (page 172) templates. These put emphasis on your personal statement, skills, and educational achievements, rather than on your work history.

And finally, although there are many advertised roles that require experience, there are also plenty that don't. It's worth setting your sights at a realistic level to begin with – starting small and having the tenacity to work your way up will pay rich dividends in the future. Every expert started out as a beginner once.

You think you're too young or too old

Applicants and recruiters can hold assumptions about the 'correct' age for a job title. Marketing executives are young and lively, heads of department are over 40, and if you're the Pope – well, the sky's the limit. It's all nonsense, of course, but that's little comfort when you're convinced that you're either too young or too old for your CV to be taken seriously. These issues are one of the reasons why it's now against the law (in the UK at least) for a recruiter to take an applicant's age into account. The Equality Act (2010), which came into force in 2012, makes it unlawful to discriminate against employees or trainees on the basis of age unless there are justifiable reasons for doing so. A general perception that a role is generally seen as a young or old person's job is not one of them.

You think

I know it's against the law to take age into account, but still, is there any point in me applying for this job when they'll probably think I'm too young/too old for it? How can I use my CV to reassure them that age isn't an issue?

The recruiter thinks

From what I can see of this person's education and experience, I'm not sure that they have enough under their belt to warrant an interview. Alternatively: from what I can see of this person's education and experience, they look to be in their fifties. Why are they applying for a young person's job, and will they want to retire soon? It looks a bit fishy to me.

Your CV strategy

Take age off the table. If you think you'll be considered to be too young, and you're convinced you've accomplished enough to be taken seriously, highlight what you've done. If you think you'll be considered too old, consider your experience as an asset, but show you still have the energy and ambition to make a success of the role.

Top-line tactics

Don't be defensive about your age, or mention it in either your CV or cover letter, for example by entering your date of birth. Recruiters don't want to be in a position where they're accused of discrimination. Naturally they'll be able to judge your approximate age by looking at the dates of your education and employment, but that's as far as it should go.

Generally speaking, recruiters aren't ageist but they can be 'energist'. In other words, they might assume that a younger candidate has more passion to give to the job, so use your personal statement to emphasise your enthusiasm for the role. If you're a young applicant take care to write it with a level of gravitas, and if you're an older one you'll want to show vitality and enthusiasm. There's no need to use anything other than the basic reverse-chronological CV format, which most recruiters prefer in any case (see page 166) The last thing you want is to come across as hiding your work history.

Be proud of your age and the advantages it gives you. Yes, you may have to overcome some innate prejudice (hiring managers are human, just like the rest of us), but the less you let it bother you, the more likely you are to come across in a positive way.

You want a part-time or flexible role

Whether you want to combine work with childcare, have time for an important hobby, or even hold another job on the side, recruiters are used to applicants asking for flexibility. You wouldn't think it to look at the job adverts, though, would you? The vast majority seem to be for full-time roles, with only a smattering specifying flexibility or part-time hours. And having the right to request this only applies to you if you're an internal candidate with at least 26 weeks' service. So if you've seen a job you'd love to have, but you want to do it on your terms, how do you craft your CV so it reflects that without putting the recruiter off?

You think

That job would be perfect for me, but only if I can do it three days a week. It's a dilemma – do I say that in my CV or cover letter, or do I apply without mentioning it and hope I can negotiate it later?

The recruiter thinks

If I see one more applicant asking for flexible hours at the interview, or even worse when they're offered the job, I will ... (cue unmentionable word).

Your CV strategy

If a compromise on hours is important to you, it's best to put this in your CV or cover letter. Don't leave it until you meet the hiring manager or are offered the job. Some roles come with built-in flexibility and others don't – it all depends on the organisation, the nature of the work, and the company culture.

Top-line tactics

Use your personal statement to briefly say you're looking for a part-time or flexible role, and give an indication of what level of hours you're looking for. Your cover letter is also a great place to put this, as you'll have the chance to add in more detail there. Plus, it's helpful if you explain why, as that gives the recruiter more to go on. Wherever you put it, though, don't make it the number one point. Add it into the last sentence of your personal statement. You want your skills and experience to be noticed more than the hours you want to work.

> *'A personal statement is a good synopsis because often recruiters will look at someone's job titles, then in their personal statement they'll find they're actually looking for something different, or for part-time work.*
> *So your personal statement is your chance to say what you've done, what you've achieved, and what you're looking to do next.'*

Try our part-time CV template (see page 176) for size, and consider this example of how you could word your personal statement:

Example: 'An experienced office administrator, with over six years' admin experience. Examples of my success include improving the efficiency of my current organisation through implementing new indexing and filing systems. I also have a wealth of experience in liaising with multiple stakeholders around the business on a number of different projects. I am currently studying for my EA Diploma, and looking for a part-time position to complement my schedule. I am extremely flexible with regards to working hours.'

You're not working at the moment

There are many legitimate reasons why you might not have a job right now: redundancy or being on a career break are the two most common ones. This can spark a crisis of confidence when it comes to your CV. Suddenly your employment history section, which seemed to pose so few problems when you were in work before, has become a minefield. What should you put as your reason for leaving? How can you best explain why you're not working at the moment? This uncertainty can make it daunting to launch yourself into the job-hunting game.

You think

What's the best way of explaining my lack of work without putting employers off? I don't want to look like a loser.

The recruiter thinks

So they're out of work right now. I wonder why? Proceed with caution.

> 'The worst CV I've ever seen had reasons for leaving and they were really negative. He was making excuses for everything.'

Your CV strategy

Generally, a recruiter is more interested in what you've done before and can do in the future, rather than what you're doing right now – as long as they know why you're out of work. A lack of explanation will come across as suspicious. So if you were made redundant, was it because of a corporate restructure, a cost-saving exercise, or some other reason? Giving a short and simple explanation can work wonders. After all, a hiring manager would need to have their head stuck up a drainpipe not to know that being made redundant is hardly headline news these days. And career breaks are no sin either, as long as there's a just cause.

> *'I've worked with the long-term unemployed, and*
> *obviously they'll focus on skills-based CVs. But most*
> *recruiters prefer reverse-chronological.'*

Top-line tactics

Your main focus should be on your employment history and skills, just as it would be if you were in work already. A good place to mention your current situation is in your personal statement, but don't dwell on it – your CV is for the positive points, not the negative. You can use these two examples for inspiration:

Redundancy example: 'A driven retail manager with over ten years' experience in the fashion industry, I have a proven track record of success which includes managing the top-performing store in the region, and having the lowest staff turnover rate of all UK outlets. Currently out of work due to company closure, I am looking for the right opportunity to bring my expertise to a well-established fashion brand in an upper-management position.'

Career-break example: 'A highly motivated and experienced PA, looking to resume my professional career after dedicating the last five years to raising a family. I have excellent admin skills, thorough knowledge of all Microsoft Office programmes, as well as proficiency in minute-taking and extensive experience liaising with clients. After volunteering for one day a week with a local charity to refresh my skills, I am now fully committed to continuing my career on a full-time basis.'

If you've been unemployed for a while, you can also use your bullet points to talk about what you've been doing in that time. Any voluntary work or retraining should go in here, and you can even create a new 'job' for it if your activities are significant. Try the redundancy or career-break CV templates to guide you (see pages 178 and 174) – you'll see in the career-break one that you start with your skills rather than your employment history, but you can switch these around if your break hasn't been that long. Alternatively, mention your situation in your cover letter instead.

You have something to hide

Many jobseekers are worried about some aspect of their life or work history, and would rather it didn't make an appearance in their CV. Hopefully, having read the above scenarios, you'll feel reassured by the most common ones. But what if there really is a skeleton in your closet? We're talking criminal records or being sacked by a previous boss – the kind of events you almost certainly regret and would rather forget, but which an employer sometimes has the right to know about.

'Someone wrote on their CV that they'd left their previous company "on bed terms" rather than "bad terms". Intriguing!'

You think

I know I can do this job and I'm certain I will play straight with it, but how will I ever be considered for an interview when I have this stain on my record?

The recruiter thinks

Criminal record? Fired from a job? This person's going on the reject pile unless they can convince me they're worth meeting.

Your CV strategy

It depends how much time has gone by since the event in question. If it's a criminal record that you're worried about, in the UK the Rehabilitation of Offenders Act (1974) means that some minor offences are considered 'spent', or ignored after a set period of time, so as far as job applications go, you can act as if it never happened. What's more, a recruiter isn't legally allowed to ask you if you have a spent conviction, nor can they refuse you an interview if you have one. The exception to this is if it can be justified in the context of the role, such as working with children, vulnerable people, or in certain professions. Convictions are considered spent after the following time periods (although this list isn't exhaustive):

- For a simple or youth caution: immediately spent
- For a conditional caution: three months
- For a prison sentence under six months: the length of the sentence plus two years
- For one more than six months and under 30 months: the length of the sentence plus four years
- For one more than 30 months and under four years: the length of the sentence plus seven years
- For one more than four years: never (this means that if your conviction resulted in a prison sentence of more than four years you'll still have to disclose it if asked, regardless of how long ago it was)

Top-line tactics

A good number of employers help to rehabilitate former prisoners and are happy to consider applications from them, so all is not lost. Having said that, there's no need to mention your criminal record on your CV or cover letter if you're not asked, even if it's one that isn't spent. But if you're questioned about it at a later stage, or if you're completing an application form which demands to know about it, you need to disclose it if it falls within the rules. Likewise, you're not obliged to explain why you left any job. You'll need to be honest if asked about it in an interview, but otherwise don't dwell upon it. For CV tips, you'll find the above section 'You're not working at the moment' helpful.

Your main task here is to emphasise the enthusiasm you have for the job, the skills, and experience you possess, and the strong intention you have not to repeat the error of your ways. Use your bullet points to showcase what you've achieved since that time, especially if they indicate that you're trustworthy and honest. And bear in mind that some employers are open-minded about hiring people with convictions, as long as they're honest about it.

SUMMING UP

By now you should be reassured that no challenge is insurmountable when it comes to creating your CV. You just need to bear in mind the seven-second rule: make sure you're creating an impact, that your strengths jump out, and that your issue seems like a minor consideration.

But what if you're going for a job in an industry that has its own unwritten rules for CVs – how should you approach your application then? That's what we'll cover in the next chapter.

CHAPTER 7

CVs for Specific Sectors

Remember your first day in your current job? You probably felt like a fish out of water. Everyone seemed to know what to do and when, while you were stuck trying to locate the stationery cupboard or finding out who to ask about your tax code. But as always happens, you settled in eventually, and probably only realised you had when the next newbie joined and asked you where the staplers were kept. It's easy when you know how it works, isn't it?

> *'I once received a CV from a contract manager who worked within the "Public Sector" but put "Pubic Sector" on his CV.'*

Just as individual workplaces have their own unwritten rules, it's the same for CVs when you're applying for a job in selected industries and sectors. A seemingly baffling set of assumptions has evolved, which can make you feel at a disadvantage if you're new to the field. And it's just as much of a pitfall if you've been working in that sector forever, because – just like with anything else in life – customs change, which means that what might have been best practice a few years ago may not impress a recruiter now.

This comes into play when you're wanting your CV to pass the seven-second test in any of these industries:

- *The professions:* these are highly regulated areas of work, and demand specific levels of training and qualifications as a minimum requirement for entry. The 'classic' professions are law, medicine, accountancy, and teaching. However, some other careers also have a need for specialised training, such as nursing, HR, and social work.
- *The creative sectors:* for these, a recruiter will want to see a portfolio of some kind, and possibly a different approach to design in your CV.
- *Academia or the research sectors:* for roles in these you'll need to showcase your qualifications and the publications you've authored or contributed to.

It would be a terrible shame for your carefully crafted CV to land in the reject pile, all because of rules you didn't know you were breaking, so let's look at each sector in turn. Here's the catch, though: just because you know what to do, it doesn't mean you should aim to blend in with everyone else. Your industry may have its expectations, but it still wants applicants that shine. Everything you've learned so far about writing a stand-out CV still applies, you just need to apply the sector-specific rules to it.

PROFESSIONAL CVS

All professions demand some kind of qualification as a basic requirement for gaining an interview, with preference given to candidates who've achieved above and beyond. This isn't only the case for the classic professions, either – in some other professional jobs a qualification is often asked for, such as the CIPD for human resources managers. Your key tactic here is to make sure that yours can be seen within the first seven seconds of a hiring manager clicking 'open'. There's nothing more frustrating for them than having to hunt to find your accountancy or medical degree hidden at the end of your CV along with your A-Level results – don't put a recruiter in a bad mood, it's never a great idea. Also, bear in mind that membership of your professional body can be as much of a basic requirement as having the right level of training, so include that too.

> *'In accountancy roles, if you're a graduate you should put if you're experienced in Sage or Excel. If that's at the top, it's going to be a hook.'*

Why not add the initials your qualification gives you the right to use after your name at the top of your CV? So 'Mohammed Baqri' becomes 'Mohammed Baqri, PGCE', and 'Sheila Jones' becomes 'Sheila Jones, ACA'. Always put the highest-level versions of your qualification and memberships there, or add them one after the other: 'Sheila Jones, ACA, CIMA'. It may not be strictly conventional to add qualifications when they're under a doctorate level, but it's worth trying.

Next, mention your qualification in your personal statement so that it's right at the beginning of your CV.

Example: 'A fully qualified chartered accountant with seven years' experience, I am a member of the Chartered Institute of Management Accountants (CIMA)'.

You can even consider replacing your personal statement with a bulleted list of your qualifications if they're particularly impressive or important.

> *'For accountancy, actuarial, or anything where you need to be qualified, put "qualified" or "part qualified" at the top, then the discipline within that (like tax or life insurance). So you need four or five bullet points at the top of that CV that show the specialisms you're qualified in and are relevant. This is more important than a general personal statement.'*

A danger to avoid, which many professionals fall into, is the over-use of jargon. Notice how, in the example above, this candidate doesn't assume that the hiring manager knows what CIMA means. That recruiter might be a consultant who recruits people for all sorts of jobs, not just the profession in question. At the same time, though, you want to show that you understand the industry. Use enough of the right technical words to prove this, but not so many that you'll confuse people. When you're thinking about what terms to use you'll also want to remember the Applicant Tracking System, through which your CV will quite likely be passed in order to filter out candidates. The job advert will tell you which sector-specific qualifications are required, so make sure that you replicate them in your CV, and expand on any initials you use, as our example applicant did above.

Another pitfall for the professional applicant is being too general when talking about your work history. You can't assume that hiring managers will know what 'three years as an A&E doctor' involves, so be specific enough to give them a flavour of what you've done. Outline how many beds the hospital had, whether or not it was a teaching hospital, how many staff you worked with, and the extent of your responsibilities. That way you're building a vivid picture of your experience. Also, highlight any special achievements or projects you successfully completed – you're wanting to stand out, not look as if you're only as well qualified as all the other candidates.

In terms of your CV format, you'll want to start with your personal statement, then move to a bulleted list of your qualifications. You can also include work-related training in here, as well as your years of experience, if that plays to your strengths. After that comes your work history, then your skills, and finally your school-level education. Try our template on page 166 to make it easier.

Finally, your LinkedIn profile is important and will almost certainly be checked out by a recruiter. Is it up to date? Would someone reading it see that it's for the same person who wrote the CV? If not, you'll raise doubts in their mind. The same goes for any other social media profiles you have – make sure that they present a consistent, professional, and competent image of yourself.

> 'We advise people, particularly if they are professional
> or semi-professional, to have a really good
> LinkedIn account and be very careful about
> what they post on other sites.'

CREATIVE CVS

If you visit St John's Co-Cathedral in Valletta, Malta, you'll come across one of the most unusual CVs you're likely to see. It's a painting called *St George on Horseback* by Mattia Preti, which the artist submitted as a 'prove-it' piece before being commissioned by the Knights of Malta to paint the whole ceiling of the cathedral. Creatives have been submitting samples of their work for as long as there have been people willing to pay for it – even in the seventeenth century, CV portfolios were alive and well.

> 'If you're working in marketing or creative then it's
> appropriate to have links to your website. If you're a
> graphic designer you can include a link that takes
> you to a website you've created.'

When you apply for a creative role, whether it be related to visual art, design, performing arts, the media, or any other similar field, hiring managers will want to assess the work you've done before because they see it as an indication of what you'll produce in the future. So what's the best way to submit your CV to someone in the creative industries? First of all, look at the job advert for guidance – if a portfolio is requested in a particular format, for instance, give the recruiter what he or she wants, not what you think is best.

Next, think about how you're going to craft the CV itself. The advice is different if you're applying for a visually creative role as opposed to another, so this section is split in two.

1. CVs for visual creatives

If you're an artist, graphic designer, director, photographer, illustrator, architect, or anyone applying for a role based on visual creativity, here's where you can let your creative juices flow, within reason. Remember, this is still a job application, not a bid to create the next Picasso masterpiece. Recruiters for visually creative roles will expect to see you putting your skills into practice in your CV (unless they've specified in the job advert not to), but they still want to skim it quickly and extract the key details without any trouble. This challenge shouldn't be unsurmountable for a designer, should it?

The best approach is to take the CV format that works best for you, and then to add your genius to it. That way you're starting from a sound basis, but you're also standing out as a creative individual. Alternatively – and only you can know if this is a good idea for the particular company you're applying to – you can throw out the rule book and go wild. It's a risk, but as long as you've included all the elements the recruiter has asked for, you may strike gold.

'For creative roles I would use a design CV because it's almost like your business card. If we were searching for CVs for this kind of role we'd know we might have to go into the ATS system and manually open some of the CVs.'

Inherent in any application will be the need to include a portfolio of your work. If the job advert specifies how to provide it then go with what's been requested, but if not, it's best to include a link to an online portfolio in your work history section. Luckily there are some great online platforms for you to do this, such as Behance, Wix, Squarespace, Format, and more. Pick the most impressive ten or twenty examples of your experience, making sure that you showcase a variety of skills if possible. What kind of creative work will be expected of you in this role? Choose the pieces that most closely reflect them. Also, highlight the results gained from them, either on your CV or within the portfolio itself. Was there a particular challenge involved? Did it achieve an impressive result? Adding in these details may be what sets you apart from the other candidates, because employers want results, not just pretty pictures. If you've not had much work history, consider developing some sample pieces to fill up your portfolio (labelling them as such, of course).

Having said all this, fortune favours the brave in the world of job applications and there's always room for a maverick. My cousin once applied for a job in a TV production company, and instead of sending in a standard CV, created an A4-size cartoon storyboard using his own illustrations. This showcased his creativity and skills as an illustrator. He got the job!

2. CVs for other creatives

If you're an actor, dancer, writer, or any other creative whose work isn't so easily shown visually on the page, you should take a more conservative approach to the design of your CV. Recruiters much prefer a standard Word document with the information laid out in the way they're expecting, because it's what they're used to and it's compatible with applicant tracking systems. They often make exceptions for visual creatives, but are less likely to do so for anyone else.

'You should be able to back up every single thing on your CV. We've had developers say they can use

*Javascript and we've sat them down in the interview and
asked them to use it, and they can't.'*

However, they still want to see examples of what you can do
in the form of a portfolio, and how you show this depends on
your area of expertise. If you're in the performing arts or film,
then a series of video links to your YouTube channel or personal
website would work well, whereas if you're a writer you could
send a PDF of writing samples along with your CV, or provide a
link to where they can be found online. Include these in the work
history section of your CV.

ACADEMIC AND RESEARCH CVS

If you're applying for an academic or research-based job it's easy
to assume that your qualifications, together with the publications you've authored or contributed to, are what will set you
apart. It's true, these are vital because they show the breadth
and depth of your expertise, but they're not necessarily what
employers most value. They take for granted that you know a
lot, but they want to see that you can do a lot too. So show how
you could contribute to their institution in additional ways, such
as through the successful implementation of projects, leading a
team, or making lucrative grant applications. You can see from
this that the rules for an academic or research CV are much the
same as for any other – showcase your work history, achievements, mindset qualities, and skills over anything else.

*'It really bugs me when people have pages and pages of
education, but not the experience they have.'*

Also, academics tend to have (sometimes unfairly) a reputation for being overly wordy, as if they're communicating only
with their peers. That's fine when you're writing your thesis,

but not when you're crafting your CV, and it usually stems from professional pride. You're not writing your magnum opus here, but a hard-working sales document to showcase your skills and experience. To strike the right tone, find out who'll be the first person to screen your CV. Especially if it's a recruiter who isn't an expert in your field, you need to be convincing in ways you might not be used to. Replace long words with shorter ones, write in the first person, and keep your written voice active rather than passive. Use punchy, powerful bullet points and plenty of white space between each section. Your aim here is to land an interview, not to impress other experts in your field, so don't give the recruiter an opportunity to dismiss you along with all the rest.

> 'Having a LinkedIn profile is useful because there are lots of articles shared on there, and I would think that people who are on the site are more aware of current situations in their industry and specialism.'

In terms of your CV format, start in the usual way with your personal statement, work history, and skills. Then include a list of your publications and research projects in a separate section. That way, those who are interested can look them up, and those who can't tell the difference between an asteroid and an aphelion won't be turned off. If you like, try out our template to help you (see page 166). And finally, a refresh of your LinkedIn profile wouldn't go amiss – make sure it's up to date and reflects what's on your CV.

If you think there are bespoke rules for your own industry or sector that we've not covered here, I'd love to hear about them. Email me at james.reed@reed.co.uk and let me know. And now that we've dealt with the details of CVs in different industries, let's look at what else you can do to put yourself in the interview chair. This is where it gets even more exciting!

CHAPTER 8

What Else Can You Do to Put Yourself in the Interview Chair?

Picture the scene. It's a drizzly Monday morning at Media Services 'R' Us; an HR manager arrives in the office after braving the rush-hour traffic. She sighs as she sips a much-needed coffee, then flips open her laptop and eyes the influx of CVs from over the weekend. Clicking on the first one, she scrolls down and sees nothing which grabs her attention. The second is the same. But on the third, her boss sees her sit up straight and a smile creep onto her face. Not only is that CV beautifully worded and laid out (making her life so much easier), but it also includes links to the candidate's social profiles and personal website at the top. This is getting more interesting ...

As you'll have discovered by now, there are many ways to create a CV that grabs a recruiter's attention and keeps him or her reading to the end. Layout and content are fundamental to this, but what about the other steps you can take to be noticed? You're more than just two sides of A4, after all, so why not show the world what you're really made of by building a professional profile online? For hiring managers, it's like the difference between watching a movie with the sound off and then turning it on – suddenly they're looking at a whole person, rather than a cardboard cut-out.

YOUR DIGITAL FOOTPRINT

The purpose of your online activity in a job-hunting context is to add weight and authenticity to your CV, rounding you out as a person and showing what you're truly about. There's no better way to do this than by using social media and, possibly, your own personal website – this is what's known as your 'digital footprint'. Think of this as a support to your CV, fleshing out what's on the page. It's reassuring for recruiters when they can see more about you, and if they like what they discover they'll be more inclined to offer you an interview. My crowdsourced research with hiring managers revealed that 14 per cent of them always look up candidates on social media after receiving their CV, and 44 per cent often do. This isn't an area you can ignore.

There's another side to this. We've all heard the horror stories about people who were considered for jobs, only for the offer to be snatched away as soon as the recruiter saw the full reality of their personal lives displayed across a computer screen. This can happen at any stage of the recruitment process, from being considered for an interview, to being offered the job, and even when you're actually doing it. This is easily avoided. Take the example of an applicant for a role at a large employer, who tweeted that their interview preparation consisted of memorising the exaggerations they'd made on their CV so they wouldn't trip themselves up. It was forwarded to the hiring manager, with predictable results.

'I encourage people to have a look at their digital footprint.'

This is an extreme case and can be circumvented with the application of some old-fashioned common sense, but how do you create a powerful and positive online presence for yourself that enhances your CV? It's not quite as simple as uploading a couple of social profiles and leaving them to wither on the web. Nor is it a great idea to pull together a personal website that doesn't do justice to you as a person. It's a good idea to develop a habit of Googling yourself once in a while (using an incognito window if you're in Chrome, as it gives you an objective view of your results). Do you like what you see? If not, what can you do about it? It might be an unflattering photo a friend posted of you on social media, in which case you can ask them to take it down. If that's not possible, the more 'correct' content you produce from now on, the quicker that unfavourable shot will sink without a trace. 27 per cent of the recruiter respondents to our survey said they'd rejected a CV because of what was on the candidate's social media profile – it's not a risk worth taking.

'I always Google candidates.'

At this point, it's worth mentioning that none of this is compulsory. It's unlikely your CV would be rejected purely on the basis of your having no digital footprint, unless you're applying for the kind of job where you'd be expected to have one. But think of the competition your CV is facing out there. When we advertise for people to work with us, we regularly receive hundreds of applications per role. That's not the case for every opening you'll be going for, but the more you can do to shine online, the better. At the very least, make sure that you're not harming your prospects by putting the wrong stuff out there.

Let's look at what it takes to harness the power of digital in service of your CV, by taking the basic principles of savvy social networking and then examining each platform in turn. We'll also consider the benefits of having your own personal website.

YOUR PERSONAL BRAND

When you think about the brands you love, you'll find yourself having a positive emotional reaction to them. We've all gone out of our way to buy our favourites when easier and cheaper versions were closer to hand, because we want the best and 'AN Other' isn't good enough. Isn't that what you'd want a recruiter to do for you? The phrase 'personal brand' will either excite you or make you shudder, but in a digital sense, all it means is the sum of what recruiters think and feel about you when they see you online. This includes your social media profiles, your personal website (if you have one), and any information about you that can be gleaned through a search. Your CV doesn't exist in a vacuum – it's just one piece of the jigsaw that makes up 'Brand You'. Because not only does having a strong, positive image help your CV wing its way onto the 'yes' pile, but it also paves the way for your interview to go well, and eventually for you to negotiate a favourable package should you be offered the job.

'Who doesn't Google search people? We would Google someone, look at images, then probably the top five articles that come up.'

Steps to creating a professional personal brand

If you think you don't have a personal brand, you're wrong. You have a personality, experience, skills, and strengths – all of which add up to an image, even if you might not see it like that. The problem is, it's probably not consistent. Ask your friends what kind of person you are, and you'll be told one thing. Ask your family, and you'll hear something else. Your current colleagues may say something different again. Like it or not, many recruiters view how you present yourself socially online as more reflective of your true character than what you say about yourself on your CV. What you therefore need is a way of presenting yourself that joins the dots between your various profiles, so that any recruiter looking at your CV and then checking you out online would see the connection between who you say you are on paper and who you reveal yourself to be in practice. Here are the steps to take to make sure your brand is consistent:

1. Stop thinking of yourself as a potential member of staff, but instead as an asset to an organisation. What value can you bring that would be needed and appreciated? What do you have to offer?

2. Who are you, professionally speaking? Are you well qualified and career focused, or organised and practical? You may be a bit of both, but now's the time to decide on your main strengths and characteristics, because you'll be basing your brand on these going forward. You can use the skills you identified on page 57 as a starting point.

3. Find your ideal online platforms to develop your brand (you'll learn more about these in a moment).

4. Craft your social profile bios to reflect who you are at your best and most professional. Remember, you're 'Super You' online.

5. When you post on those profiles be yourself, but the kind of self you'd be happy for a recruiter to see.

Let's take a look at the activities for steps 3–5 in more detail.

Arrange a decent headshot

This is particularly important for your profile picture on LinkedIn and Twitter. Many jobseekers use a selfie or a photo a friend took of them, which is often not the most professional look. You want a clear photograph of you (and only you – no cropped-out people behind you) from the shoulders up, with a plain background. Avoid sunglasses and hats, and wear something that looks similar to what you'd wear to an interview. If you possibly can, hire a local photographer to take some flattering professional head shots – they're probably more affordable than you think, and you can use them again and again. If that's not an option, ask a friend to snap you in a suitably professional mode.

For other social platforms you can be more casual with your profile picture, but make sure it wouldn't embarrass you if a recruiter was to see it.

Write your profile

How you do this depends on the platform, but your main aim is to imagine what impression you're making on the recruiter reading it. Is it clear what you're good at, and how you can contribute to an organisation? What kind of person do you come across as?

Follow and connect with others

Generally, the users you're connected to are visible to anyone looking at your profile. Recruiters will want to see you're following the right people, so if you're gunning for a job in publishing and you're a Twitter user, make sure you're following the major writers and editors on there. It shows you're in with the right crowd and, you never know, some may follow you back. You'll also be picking up on the latest news from the field, which is something that will come in handy for your cover letter and interview.

Create your posts

Your profile goes some way towards showcasing your personality, but it's your posts that highlight who you are. Again, this depends on the platform, but you want to put yourself across as being professional and pleasant – the sort of person that any recruiter would love to have along for an interview. This is not to suggest that you shouldn't post anything personal (unless it's on LinkedIn) – social media is meant to be fun, after all – but just be mindful of the impression you're making.

Drumming up ideas for what to post can have you racking your brains. As you learn to be more proficient with this it will become easier, but you can also link to other people's posts or curate content you find across the internet. It shows that you're in touch with the trends, and is helpful for your audience as well. It's good to have an active presence on social media. You'll be more visible to hiring managers, and also be showing that you're proactive in keeping up to date with your industry.

Once you've decided which platforms to include, enter the links to them at the top of your CV after your contact details.

SOCIAL MEDIA PLATFORMS

Now let's move onto the individual platforms and how to use them to build your personal brand. Think of it as if you were marketing yourself as a company, which you can think of as Me PLC.

LinkedIn

If there's ever a social site that recruiters pay attention to, it's LinkedIn – in fact my research showed that 58 per cent of them look at it the most. It's designed for people to connect profession-ally and to showcase their expertise, so it goes without saying that you should consider having a presence on there, no matter what kind of job you're looking for. Recruiters regularly look people up on LinkedIn in order to compare what they see on the person's CV with their profile – in fact, if you Google your name you'll probably find that it's your LinkedIn profile that comes up first, even before your own personal website. If your CV and your LinkedIn profile are mismatched, hiring managers will feel at best confused and at worst suspicious, so aligning your profile with your CV is vital. This is tricky if you're going for a career change, which means that it's a good idea to be up front about this on your CV or cover letter.

For your LinkedIn profile, a clear, professional headshot and a snappy 'headline' are key. Your headline is the line that goes beneath your picture and describes what you do. Use it to explain this in a way that makes sense to others, rather than just you, and be specific. So if you're a marketing manager, put that down rather than 'corporate executive'. Recruiters often search LinkedIn by key word, so think of two or three words they might use and make sure they're in your headline and profile description.

> *'I sometimes use LinkedIn, because there have been discrepancies at times. I say to people, "Hang on, your CV says this but your LinkedIn profile says something different."'*

In your description you can use more words than in your personal statement on your CV. Write it in the first person, and use it to outline your experience and what you have to offer an organisation. A good structure to base it on is this:

- ***Who you are:*** 'A marketing manager with five years' experience in blue chip companies' (then go on to outline your main achievements).
- ***What you do:*** 'I plan and implement complex digital campaigns' (then go into more detail on your key responsibilities).

If you're currently out of work, you can add the fact that you're looking for specific types of roles at the end of your description (do they match your CV?). If you're in work, though, you'll probably want to keep your job search under your hat rather than broadcast it to your boss.

A key part of your profile is your endorsements and recommendations. There's nothing more interesting to a recruiter than what others say about you, as opposed to what you say about yourself. Consider who you could approach to give you a good recommendation, and send them the LinkedIn link to do so. Past managers, current colleagues, and those who you've impressed outside of work all qualify. Endorsements are also a bonus.

> '*I wouldn't be put off by a candidate who didn't have a LinkedIn profile, but it's an advantage if they do. It makes things easier.*'

Finally, complete your experience section, using the work history information you compiled for your CV. It's important to make sure that it's complete, because having a gap in your experience will arouse suspicion. You want to show the full breadth of what you've done, so don't skimp on this part. Also, you should include volunteer work, especially if you have little work history.

Building up connections is one of the main benefits of being on the platform, because it opens up your connections' connections to you. This expands your network exponentially, and makes it more likely that a recruiter will see your full profile. There are various ways you can search on the site for people you know, so send out a few connection requests. If they accept, you're connected, which means you'll see their updates in your feed and can message them – and vice versa.

In terms of posting, LinkedIn gives you the opportunity to create and share posts and articles. You don't have to do this, but if you're able to showcase your expertise in this way, all the better. One of our recruiters found a chef on LinkedIn, who used the platform to post pictures of his cake creations. He was given an interview partly because they looked so delicious. Don't underestimate the power of rounding out your profile by posting relevant work activity, and joining a few groups related to your area of work. If you're seen to be taking steps to keep yourself up to date with your industry it can only make you look good – as well as giving you additional material for your cover letter and interview.

> *'I knew I was hired before I was officially told, because I got 12 different views on LinkedIn.'*

A word about privacy: if you're wanting to keep your job search under your hat, a suddenly revamped profile, together with a rash of connections with recruiters, is a dead giveaway. You can tailor your security settings so that your profile updates aren't broadcast to all, but don't make it completely private – you want recruiters to be able to access it easily.

> *'If you're not prepared to change anything on your social media accounts, at least check your privacy settings.'*

Twitter

While most recruiters won't pay as much attention to your Twitter account as they will to LinkedIn, it's easy to underestimate it as a way of showing hiring managers who you 'really are'. You can expect your Twitter feed to come under particular scrutiny if you're applying for a job in the media, marketing, or entertainment industries, because they'll want to see if you're being smart with it.

Your headshot should follow the same guidelines as LinkedIn, although you have the freedom to be a bit more relaxed on Twitter. When you're writing your bio and tweeting your posts, think carefully about the impression you're creating. Many people use Twitter for personal reasons as well as to create a professional image, so there's no need to keep your conversation purely work related, but try to strike a balance. How about this for a sample bio: 'Record-breaking sales manager, dreams of playing football for England'. You're allowed to add a link to a website in your bio – why not make it your LinkedIn profile, or your personal website if you have one? While you're about it, make sure your Twitter handle doesn't give the wrong impression: @SexyBoy or @WineLover33 don't exactly put you in a professional light. You can change your Twitter handle if you've already set it up, so pick something based on your name instead.

Having thousands of followers isn't necessary if you're using Twitter to bolster your CV, but it's nice to have a few hundred at least. You attract followers by following people, so find users who are in your field by browsing Twitter lists of industry influencers and people in your email address book, and try your luck. You can also search for key words related to your work field, and find people that way. You'll succeed most easily if you're somebody worth following yourself, which means tweeting items of interest related to your expertise, or funny stuff about your job and personal life (as long as it doesn't reflect badly on you).

> *'My CV includes links to my LinkedIn and Twitter, but not everyone is proud of what's on their Twitter account.'*

Twitter is all about engagement. It takes time to build a following – be prepared to spend a few months at it before you see significant results – but you can start replying to and re-tweeting people straight away. Nobody posts on Twitter to be ignored, so don't be shy about jumping into conversations. You want to be noticed and come across as proactive and helpful.

Finally, if you're openly job seeking, you can use your Twitter bio and your tweets to show you're looking for work in a certain area. You never know who might see it.

Facebook

We could hardly talk about social media without mentioning Facebook. However, as you're sure to know, it's mainly used for social reasons. Recruiters won't be looking at it to judge how well you know your industry or what your opinions are about your work, but they might take a peek at your profile to see if you're the kind of person they'd like to have working with them. In fact, 32 per cent of the recruiters we asked said that if they were to look at a candidate's social profiles, Facebook would be one of them. Unfortunately, if your page is plastered with pictures of you ... well ... plastered, it's not been unknown for CVs that would have gone into the 'yes' pile to be swiftly relocated to 'never in a million years'.

> *'I do advise people to go onto their Facebook account and write down three or four adjectives about their profile.'*

Your best bet is to set your account to private and keep your privacy settings up to date, so only your Facebook friends can see the content. Bear in mind, though, that your photos will still be visible, as will any that circulate around the network that you're tagged or mentioned in.

YouTube

Creating a video is a quick and effective way to get your point across to a recruiter, because it gives you the chance to answer the most common interview question: 'tell me about yourself'. It isn't for everyone, but depending on the type of job you're applying for, YouTube can be a fantastic way to stand out. So how do you go about creating a professional brand image as a jobseeker on the platform? It worked for Justin Bieber in his early days – he posted some homespun videos of himself on the channel and, after building a follower base, was spotted by a manager. Could that be you?

First make sure your channel (if you already have one) is cleaned of anything that you wouldn't want a recruiter to see, such as goofy experimental videos and those on personal topics. You can set up a separate 'jobseeker' channel with its own account if you want. Then create a video in which you talk briefly about who you are and what you could bring to your chosen industry. Video works especially well if you're going for practical roles, so why not show off your skills by filming yourself doing something relevant? You want to come across as friendly, knowledgeable, and up to date. Keep it to two minutes maximum as recruiters won't spend any longer than that. Also, it doesn't need to be professionally produced – a plain background and a smartphone are all you need. Although if you're applying for a job in the media or any related field, you should certainly make use of the free production and editing tools out there to create a more professional effect.

When you're recording your video, dress professionally in the same kind of clothes that you'd wear to an interview, and edit it to smooth out any blips. Also, make sure you're well lit. You may need to film a few takes before it's right, but it will be worth it. Multiple re-takes also allow you to relax into the process so that you come across naturally. One tip is to set your videos to private, so that when you insert the link on your CV only someone with that specific link can see it. That's a handy way of keeping your job search to yourself.

'We don't reject anyone based on their online profile because we shouldn't really be judging them by that anyway.'

Blogging

If you're applying for a job that demands that you demonstrate expertise and in-depth knowledge, there's no better way to do this than by writing a blog. In fact, all the social media platforms are blogging platforms in their own way: LinkedIn allows you to post updates and articles, Twitter is for micro-blogging, Facebook is for your personal posts, and YouTube is a video-blogging facility. The difference between these and an actual blog, however, is that the latter gives you more scope to expand your content. You can create pretty much any kind of blog you want, whether it be written, image-based, or videos. The choice is yours.

The other benefit of blogging is that it helps you to come higher in the Google rankings, because search engines are partial to regularly updated sites. What's more, a recruiter searching for your name would see your social media platforms, but would be much more impressed with a blog – after all, not everyone has the tenacity and enthusiasm to commit to writing a regular piece which showcases their understanding and skills. A blog's purpose is to help people by sharing what you know, so by writing one you're positioning yourself as a knowledgeable and helpful candidate with leadership potential.

To start a blog, first decide what platform to use. There are plenty of free ones, but WordPress is a good place to begin. Next, set up the following pages on it:

- *An 'about' page.* This gives you the opportunity to showcase who you are and what you know. Make sure that it's interesting for your readers – just like your CV and cover letter, it's more about them than you. Include a professional headshot and, if you can, some other photos of yourself.
- *A contact page.* You can remove your personal details from this and just have a contact form if you like.
- *A portfolio page.* If that's relevant for you.
- *Your blog.* This is where you'll create your posts.

You might be surprised at how many extra pages you need when it's just a blog you're creating. But a blog isn't only a collection of articles, it's a showcase for you and your expertise. With this in mind, you can create a bio at the bottom of each post to highlight what you're about: 'Ellen Francis is a physicist with three years' post-graduate experience in the engineering sector. She loves blogging about the latest developments in quantum field theory, and wants to bring her practical knowledge into a research role related to atoms, photons, and electrons.'

Next, start writing some posts. Aim for a regular schedule, at least once a week if you can. Pick topics you know would impress and be of interest to your audience of recruiters (remembering it's them that you're writing for, not yourself or your colleagues). This means writing in a way they'll understand, just like you crafted your CV and cover letter for them. At first, it can be slow to attract an audience to your blog, which is why you need to boost it by posting links to it on social media. It's easy to assume that all you have to do is to write a post and then sit back, but that's only half the job. Once your post is live, tweet it, post about it on LinkedIn, and share it with people any way you know how. Don't worry if you don't receive lots of traffic, though – your main aim as a jobseeker is to provide a credible backdrop for your CV so a recruiter can see that you know what you're talking about. If you bring in other visitors, that's a bonus.

One final note on social

Whatever social platforms you do or don't throw yourself into, make sure that they're consistent with each other. Are your profile pictures clearly of the same person? (It's best if it's the same shot.) Do you talk about yourself and your work in a way that joins the dots between your profiles and your CV? If you're applying for a mixture of roles, some in your current field and some not, it's best to leave the social media links off your CV. You want to seem professional and knowledgeable. And remember, perseverance is key. Nobody gets instant results from social media or blogging. Everyone has to begin somewhere, so make a start and keep at it for a few months before you're tempted to give up.

YOUR PERSONAL WEBSITE

What's the first thing you do when you research an expensive purchase? You go online and check out the company's website. Recruiters have considerably more invested in bringing on board the right person than you do in buying a new TV, so it makes sense to consider creating one for yourself. A well-designed website showcases who you are and what you're good at. And it's not just for a designer or a web developer, but for anyone who's serious about building their personal brand online. There are, however, pros and cons to having one:

The pros

- You can include whatever elements you like: a blog, videos, a portfolio, and audio snippets.
- You can brand it so it's a close reflection of who you are.
- You own it, which means that it's not subject to the whims of a social-media platform owner.
- The act of pulling your content together, and crafting it so that it's a reflection of your best and most valuable points, is a fantastic way of exploring your potential. And if you love what you've produced, you'll find yourself sharing it with everyone who's in a position to look at your CV – it's the digital equivalent of buying a flattering new outfit or getting a knock-out haircut. A confidence booster, in other words.
- It's a handy place for recruiters to see what you're about in one fell swoop. No clicking around on scattered social profiles for them – it's all on your website.

The cons

- It takes time, and a small financial investment, to create one.
- You're responsible for keeping it maintained and running smoothly.
- If you're intimidated by technology, you may need help with setting it up.
- A neglected website or blog is worse than none at all.

Most jobseekers get by perfectly well with their CV supported by the odd social media profile, so there's nothing compulsory about having your own website. But if you're looking to work in an industry in which your personal reputation is important, you're applying for a job that requires showcasing your technical or visual skills, or you simply want to go one step further in establishing yourself as a personal brand, and you'd enjoy it (this is crucial) then these are the steps to take.

1. Buy a domain name in your name. If your name is Shaheena Bashir, it would be great to own www.shaheenabashir.co.uk. If your name isn't available, try a variation or extension such as shaheenabashir.org, or iamshaheenabashir.net.

2. Sign up for a website-building platform. These are free or low cost and give you the tools to create your own site. You may only need a single-page site, with links to your social profiles and your blog (if you have one), and some include domain registration and hosting in the package. Examples are WordPress, Squarespace, Wix, and Weebly: all offer slick, ready-made designs that you can adapt for your own needs.

3. Create a header, made up of your name and a strapline underneath: 'Emma Stephenson, Experienced Production Manager', or 'Toby Lawrence, Media Graduate and Aspiring Film Producer'. Use your superpower to make yourself stand out. You're 'Super You' here – that's you at your best – not just any old jobseeker.

4. Create an About page with your bio, that gets across what you can best offer an employer. Focus on your key skills, experience, and personal traits, just like you did when you wrote your CV. Instead of bullet points you'll want to make your writing flow in a succinct and easy-to-read way. It's all about your reader, not you.

5. If it's relevant, add a page for your portfolio or a link to a separate portfolio site.

6. Link to your social profiles – many templates give you ready-designed social buttons for this.

7. Add some photos, both of you and using stock images if needed. You can buy these cheaply online (don't take them from the internet without permission, as you could get into trouble for that).

8. Ask someone else to proofread and critique it for you.

9. Leave it a few days, then take a fresh look at your site as if you were the hiring manager: would you offer this person an interview?

10. Give yourself a pat on the back and put the url at the top of your CV!

Whatever you do, give your website some personality. It's there to show you to the world, not to be an image of the person you think you should be. Be positive and professional, but above everything else, be real and yourself.

BEYOND SEVEN SECONDS: YOU HAD MY CURIOSITY, BUT NOW YOU HAVE MY ATTENTION

Just like in your job, recruiters' workloads are not getting any lighter, which means that attention spans are shrinking when it comes to sifting through CVs. You've already done what you can to make sure your key selling points are at the top of your CV, and you've created a professional digital footprint, but is there anything else you can do to make your application stand out? Luckily for you, there is. Some job hunters find ways to make their CVs shine visually. You can even create a video CV, something that is becoming more popular with hiring managers. This might sound a bit daunting, but you'll learn how to do it the easy way here.

'I had a CV from someone who'd uploaded a photo of a dress they'd obviously been selling on eBay, instead of their own photo! I contacted her. It turned out she was a very experienced PA and a useful candidate.'

CREATIVE CVS

There are many ways to get creative with your CV, from simply adding a personal photo to going all-out for a total design revamp. Let's take a look at the options.

Adding a headshot

This is the simplest and easiest way to give your CV the personal touch so that it doesn't look like everyone else's, and is becoming more popular, especially in Continental Europe. It comes with a warning, though. My crowdsourced recruiter research revealed that a resounding 88 per cent of recruiters said candidates shouldn't include one. Why? Because they don't see it as relevant and they worry that they might be swayed by appearance. Hiring managers are human just like the rest of us, but they know it and would rather avoid the temptation. Having said that, it might be that you want to appeal to the 12 per cent who do like a photo, so decide whether or not you want to go with the crowd.

'A photo on a CV is a "no" for me. I don't want to have any preconceived ideas about the person coming in for an interview.'

Going creative

If you're applying for a role in a creative industry, you'll want to check out Chapter 7 in which you learned how to design your CV so it showcases your originality. However, if you're not the creative type but are still keen on doing something to make your CV stand out, read on.

'I once had a CV from someone who interviewed themselves on it. One of the questions he asked himself was, "What do you think your boss thinks of you?" and he said "No comment."'

There seems to be a growing trend for job hunters to feel that they should make their CV look different from the crowd. This is driven by the increase in free online tools that make this process relatively simple even if you're not a trained designer, such as infographic creation software and image manipulation packages. Should you jump on the bandwagon? If you want the short answer, it's no. If you want the long one, here goes. Most recruiters don't like design CVs unless they're for jobs in the creative industries, because they're hard to compare with others. 'And that's the very reason I'm designing mine', you cry. 'So it doesn't look like everyone else's.' But put yourself in a recruiter's shoes. They routinely sort through hundreds of CVs, and often use applicant tracking systems (ATS) to help. These systems prefer Word documents and can't read graphics or images, so you're at a disadvantage before you begin if you do go creative.

'If you're doing a design CV for a design job then fair play, but every CV comes through an ATS now so you're reducing your chances, because the system won't take it, so you're relying on the recruiter taking the extra time to read it manually.'

But here's where the human touch comes in. At some point a recruiter will look at your CV in person (assuming it passes the ATS test) and this is where design can make your CV stand out if it doesn't get in its own way. If it's hard to read, doesn't appeal to the eye of the recruiter, or messes with the standard CV formats and fonts you learned about earlier in this book, it's just not worth it unless you have a strong reason to believe it will enhance your chances. And that's something only you can decide, given the job you're going for, the organisation you're applying to, and the quality of the design skills you possess.

> 'One guy did an illustrated CV and on it were some comedic images. They weren't too bad but they were a bit close to the line, and he asked me if he should take them out. I said "No", because they show his personality. Would he want to work for a company that didn't appreciate his work? So design CVs can be good if they're clear, but you've just got to be prepared for people to say no based on that.'

At this point, it's worth recapping the three main factors that make your CV stand out for a recruiter, given the results of my research with them. I asked them the question: 'What makes a CV stand out for you?' Their answers were:

- Number one: relevant work history
- Number two: a clear visual layout
- Number three: bullet points and clear paragraphs

Can you spot anything in there to do with flashy graphics, images, stand-out colours, and innovative layouts? Neither can I.

Video CVs

Creating a video CV instead of, or in addition to, a paper one is a trend that's on the rise. There are a couple of things that have caused it. One is the explosion of social media platforms which encourage us to watch videos on a daily basis. Another is also connected to the online world, in that we use Skype, FaceTime, and other video-conferencing facilities regularly now. It was only a matter of time before recruiters started to see the benefit of assessing candidates by video. In fact, at Reed we often use video CVs, because we see this as a growing area of recruitment.

> '*I think CVs may eventually replicate social media and you'll see a picture and it'll be "swipe right if you like this person". That's what we're starting to get, where we pose questions to candidates and record them on video giving their answers. That's doing away with a CV, but we're only doing that in sectors that we know it will work in.*'

You don't have to wait until you're asked for a video CV to create one. If you want to record yourself at home talking about your experience, skills, and what you can offer a business, and then put the link on your CV, go right ahead. On the other hand, you may be asked to create one by a recruiter. If the thought of this fills you with dread, don't panic. Remember the delete button? That's the beauty of recording your CV – it's so much easier to control than when you're talking to someone face to face.

These are the steps to take in order to create a professional video CV. Most people have the equipment they need already at home, but if you don't, you're bound to have a friend or neighbour who can lend you some. You won't require much, just a phone and possibly a tripod, or failing that, a friend to hold the phone.

- **Plan your points.** Use your CV to do this, but bear in mind that you're aiming to come across as natural. So don't read from a script, but jot down the bullets and try to memorise them so you can talk around them. Keep the whole video to a minute or two.
- **Dress well.** Wear what you'd wear to an interview – you want to make a good impression.
- **Lights, camera, action!** You don't need fancy equipment, just a smartphone or home-video camera, a good light source

such as a bright lamp or window, and a plain background. If you're using your phone, turn it to landscape mode and use a tripod. Make sure there's no background noise, and if possible use a lapel mike. If you feel more energised standing up than sitting down, do it that way.

- *Just talk.* If you make a mistake at any point, delete and start again or edit it out later. You don't have to put up with second best. There's a myriad of tutorials on YouTube to help you use the free or low-cost editing tools out there.

- *Critique your video.* Does it do you justice? If you're like most people, watching yourself on screen is a bit like peeking behind your fingers at a horror film. But remember this video isn't for you but for a recruiter. Put yourself in their shoes: do you come across as likeable, professional, and enthusiastic? Have you given them a solid reason to offer you an interview? If you have, you're probably fine. Hiring managers rarely pick the video with the slickest production values or the best presentation skills (unless that's a requirement of the job). They want the person who allows their personality and best qualities to come through. Even just making the effort to create a video speaks volumes about your commitment and character.

There are so many ways to make your CV into more than a two-dimensional document. They take time, perseverance, and some creativity, but you can see how they can help it pass the seven-second test. If you're feeling overwhelmed with all this, remember that none of it's essential. Even if you just pick one social platform to excel on and include it in your CV, you'll be head and shoulders above many of your competitor candidates.

CHAPTER 9

Alternative Applications

Since time began, candidates have found weird and wonderful ways of attracting the attention of hiring managers. When I asked some of my business friends and acquaintances what were the strangest methods jobseekers had used to get their CVs in front of them, I received some hilarious replies:

'I once had a CV from what turned out to be the son of a very wealthy family delivered by hand – by their chauffeur.'

'A student sent a CV as an origami t-shirt and pants, along with a child's iron and ironing board, for a menswear design role.'

'The waiter at the local Balti knew I worked in recruitment, so decided to take the opportunity of marketing himself when delivering our Indian takeaway. I got my curry and a CV!'

'On a sandwich board on a roundabout outside my office window.'

You can't fault these jobseekers for inventiveness – they show that there are other ways of applying for jobs than simply emailing a standard CV and cover letter. However, sometimes an employer asks for a different approach themselves. We're not talking about anything radical here, simply that they might want you to upload your CV onto a job site, or to fill in an online application form. In addition, there's another way of applying for jobs that we've not looked at yet but will cover here: recruitment agencies. We'll look into how recruitment agencies can help, so that you know how to craft your CV to impress even the most demanding consultant. Let's make sure you're covering all bases.

ONLINE JOB SITES

These are online platforms – both websites and apps – that allow you to search for a job and apply for it on the spot. They're a gift to employers because they give them access to a multitude of talented job hunters like you. My favourite, unsurprisingly, is reed.co.uk. From your point of view, they allow you to search for the right job opening through the use of filters, such as location, salary, and role title. You can also use key words to focus your efforts on specific types of openings. A handy trick for these is to wrap your head around Boolean search techniques, by using the operators AND and OR when you search. Here are some examples of how this works.

- You want the job description to include multiple key words. For instance, you're after a job as a developer which allows you to use Javascript. Search for 'developer' AND 'Javascript'.
- You want the job description to include one of a number of key words, but they don't all need to appear. If you want a job

as a software developer or web developer for instance, search for 'software developer' OR 'web developer'.

- You want a job description to include an exact phrase, such as 'software developer'. Search for 'software developer' in quotation marks.
- When you want your search to start with a certain term like 'administrator', search 'admin*'. The asterisk will return all words beginning with 'admin', which will include administrators and administrative assistants.

Once you're happy with a set of search parameters, it's a good idea to create an email alert so that you're notified of suitable jobs on that site in future.

REGISTERING AND USING YOUR CV ONLINE

Most online job sites encourage you to upload your CV before you start searching. This has a few benefits: you're ready to apply for a job as soon as you see it, you're more likely to be recommended for suitable roles by the system once it can see your work history and skills, and recruiters favour those jobseekers with a fully completed profile. Naturally, you can't tailor your CV to a specific job if you do this, but you can still make sure that it's up to date and has the right key words. You should also expand on your skills as much as possible, to encourage your chances of being found by recruiters who are looking for them.

'If a candidate is uploading their CV to a job site, they need to still state the types of jobs they're applying for.'

In addition, some jobs require you to fill out an online or paper application form to apply, rather than to send in a CV and cover letter. This is where the work you've put into building your CV pays off. No plain vanilla answers for you – you already have a perfectly described catalogue of experiences, achievements, and skills.

RECRUITMENT AGENCIES

You may not need to apply for a job through a recruitment agency, but many job hunters are attracted to them because of the wide number of vacancies they have at their fingertips. If you go down this route, these tips will greatly help your chances of success.

First of all, it's helpful to understand how recruitment agencies operate. They're paid by their clients to fill job openings using the consultant's network of applicants (in other words, people like you). So they're always keen to represent the best candidates and to add them to their books if they have a suitable job for someone with your skills and experience. If they haven't, they're probably not going to be interested in you right now. Does that mean the friendly seeming consultant is really a shark in a suit? Of course not – any decent recruitment agency will help you to progress your career by putting you forward for the jobs you're most suited for. They'll also offer you advice on your CV, arrange interviews for you, negotiate your salary on your behalf if you land the job, and be a sympathetic listening ear throughout the process. This can be pretty soothing when you're in the middle of a bruising job search, and it's all for no charge. In turn, you'll be expected to turn up for an initial interview with a well-written CV which the consultant can feel confident in sending to employers, and to keep them up to date with how you're progressing. If a consultant doesn't hear from you for a while, they'll tend to assume you've landed a job independently and drop you from their call list. It's also worth knowing that recruitment agencies advertise many of their vacancies openly, so even if you're not registered with one you can still apply.

So you can see that your CV-writing skills are never wasted, even if it's not a CV you're using to apply to a specific role. In the next chapter, we'll look at what you can do to attract a recruiter's attention after – rather than before – your interview.

CHAPTER 10

Life After the CV

If you've created your 'seven-second ready' CV and it's safely in the hands of the recruiter, congratulations on a task well executed. You've already been more successful than 90 per cent of the other applicants, many of whom will have churned out a standard document and deployed a finger-crossing technique as a booster. Your CV's sole aim, however, is to win you an interview. What should you do if you're offered one, and just as importantly, if you're not? And how about a third possible scenario: crickets chirping as you wait vainly for a reply? That can be almost as bad as being turned down.

The answer to the first question is obvious: give yourself a pat on the back and pick up a copy of my book *Why You? 101 Interview Questions You'll Never Fear Again*. Just like this one, it's based on crowdsourced research with hiring managers, and lifts the lid on how to prepare for an interview so that you come out with your confidence intact and – hopefully – a job offer.

'My favourite CV mistake was, "I enjoy severing customers therefore I feel I would be a great addiction to your business."'

We'll cover the 'no' situation in a moment. For now, however, how should you respond if you don't hear anything at all? Of course, when you've sent off CVs to many companies in a short space of time, you shouldn't expect to receive feedback from all of them – that's the way it works, unfortunately. But not hearing about the one application you really care about is one of the most frustrating aspects of job hunting. You've checked your emails, made sure your phone is on loud, and conjured up a hundred possibilities for why they've not contacted you. Maybe they're busy. Maybe they've had an internal reorganisation and have withdrawn the vacancy. Maybe – and please don't let this be the case – they just don't think you're any good. What should you do? Call them to chase it up? Email them to ask what's going on? Assume they're not interested and head for the nearest box of chocolates? The answer to this conundrum is what this chapter is about: how to navigate the follow-up maze and to deal with the body blow of rejection if the news isn't good.

WHAT'S YOUR RECRUITER REALLY THINKING?

We receive thousands of applications to work at Reed every year, and our recruitment consultants deal with hundreds of candidates and employers personally. So we know a thing or two about why a recruiter might not have contacted you yet. What are the reasons?

They're playing the field

A recruiter will rarely be in a position to respond to you straight away, no matter how close a fit for the job they think you are. Just like you probably wouldn't buy the first car you see, a hiring manager will want to assess all the applicants before reaching out to potential interviewees. If it's only been a few days, or even a week or two, try to relax. It can take up to a month to receive a reply.

They're too busy

Let's put this into perspective. To you this job application is a priority, but to the recruiter it's one of many tasks. They probably have multiple roles to fill, with possibly hundreds of applications for each one. It's more than likely that your CV hasn't made it to the top of the pile for consideration yet, that's all. On the other hand the person handling yours might not be a recruitment specialist but someone doing this in addition to their day job. It's hard, but try to cut them a little slack.

They're just not that into you

To you, you're perfect for the role. But to them, not so much. Maybe your CV wasn't right, or possibly it appealed to the recruiter but not sufficiently to move you into the 'yes' pile. If you didn't do enough to set yourself apart from the other applicants, you won't be offered an interview. Some employers will let you know, and others will not contact you at all. Understandably this can seem inconsiderate and even downright rude, but look at it from their point of view: if 200 people apply and only five are interviewed, it would be enormously time consuming and costly to reply to each one. It's not right, but that's just the way it is.

So overall, it's best to acknowledge that there could be any number of valid reasons why you've been left dangling since you emailed your CV, which makes following up all the easier to do.

THE PRACTICALITIES OF FOLLOWING UP

It's all very well saying 'follow up', but what's the best way of getting in touch with busy recruiters?

Option one: email

Our survey revealed that 65 per cent of hiring managers nominate email as their preferred contact method, which makes sense when you think about how relatively non-interruptive it is. Put a few short sentences together thanking them for their time in reading your CV, and ask if there are any questions they have about it. You won't necessarily hear back from them, so if not, send a follow-up email. If nothing else this shows that you're enthusiastic. Just make sure to send it from a professional-sounding email address.

To receive a helpful response, remember to do two things: be clear about what you're asking for, and respect their time. Phrases like 'ask your advice', or 'would like some feedback' aren't as specific as they sound. The recruiter will already have read them a thousand times, and they force them to work out what you want before they can answer them. What's more, if you ask a vague question you'll receive a vague answer, and that's no use at all. Try this instead: 'I hope you received my CV which I sent on 25 November. I haven't heard back from you, so I'm attaching it again for your review. I do hope to hear from you.' Or 'Thank you for your email today in which you informed me that I haven't been selected for interview for the sales manager role. Can you tell me the main reason why? Your feedback would be useful to me and I appreciate your time.'

Option two: phone

Taking the direct approach can send shivers down the spine of even the most confident applicant, but while you might assume that calling up a recruiter would be intrusive, in certain industries it can be an excellent way to show your initiative. For sales or PR positions, for instance, hiring managers often welcome calls from candidates because it shows that they have no fear when it comes to picking up the phone. It can be as easy as asking whether they've received your application and when they're looking to make their decision. If you've been unsuccessful, ask for feedback and thank them for their time. And if they haven't made their decision yet, you've just ensured that your CV is more memorable.

Option three: social networks

If you have the name of the recruiter or you've spoken with them directly, it's perfectly acceptable to add them to your social networks. Not only is it an excellent way to keep in touch, but it's also the perfect opportunity for you to highlight how up to speed you are with your industry. So if you're able to, message them privately asking for feedback.

A caveat on timing

Just as you would sensibly wait until your boss is in a good mood before asking for a pay rise, so timing is everything when following up on a job application. In fact, it can be just as important as the method you use. Imagine a recruiter who's sifting through countless CVs – if he or she is inundated with calls a mere five minutes after the job advert has gone out, this might not go down so well. Patience is as vital as persistence for winning the interview race, so allow two or three weeks to elapse before you make a move.

WHEN NO MEANS NO

You've waited patiently, followed up if necessary, and the answer has come back as a big, fat 'no'. Welcome to the majority club. Applying for a job is a numbers game – you have to sift through a heck of a lot of topsoil before you extract any gold. You can follow all the advice in this book to the letter, and still fate can have its way with you. Maybe your CV arrived when the hiring manager was having a bad day. Possibly you weren't right for the role in the first place. Or maybe the competition was just too stiff. That's life.

First of all, don't take it personally – you can't see the other CVs. Maybe you came a close second. As you learned earlier on, success in the workplace is all about mindset. One of the three key aspects of this is 'Grit', or the determination to keep going despite setbacks. Another way of describing it is resilience. What can you learn from this rejection to increase your chances of succeeding next time? If this is a job you care deeply about, try to find out why you didn't receive an interview by calling them and asking nicely for feedback. What could you do to make your CV more compelling? Is there a step you should take in your career to give yourself a better chance next time? Did you commit any of the 'Fatal Five' mistakes? Although not all recruiters will be able to advise you, you'll be surprised at how many will set aside a little time to help. If you don't ask, you don't get, and at the very least you'll come across as proactive and interested. It might even be that your CV contained a basic error that you can quickly put right.

INTERPRETING THE FEEDBACK

Recruiters can be frustratingly opaque when they're delivering bad news, and this is largely down to human nature. None of us enjoys rejection or saying anything that sounds overly critical, so feedback is often cloaked in generic phrases. Also, your recruiter may not be someone who does this as their main profession, but who's adding to their team in a smaller company. They'll probably find it even harder to be honest. This means that you need a translator to interpret the feedback, so let's take a look at the stock phrases beloved of recruiters and what they truly mean. We'll also examine the possibility of talking the recruiter around to your point of view – it's a long shot, but at this point you've nothing to lose.

'You're overqualified'
What you hear: 'We'd rather find someone we can pay less to do the same job.'

What the recruiter means: 'We don't want you leaving after six months because you're bored.'

You have to take their point, don't you? But if you genuinely feel that you're not overqualified for the role, or if you don't see it as an issue, talk about what interests you in the company and show that you've done your research. Explain that while you may be highly qualified, you're also enthusiastic and have a lot to offer.

'You're underqualified'

What you hear: 'We expect you to have gained experience without any experience.'
What the recruiter means: 'Prove to us that it's not an issue.'

This is the phrase that everyone hates to hear, but luckily it's also a chance to prove the hiring manager wrong. Do this by talking about your best qualities (the ones that suit the role). Showing confidence in your ability to do the job can make all the difference. Never be tempted to apologise, either – if you feel the word 'sorry' is about to come out of your mouth, zip it up quick.

'We'll keep your CV on record for the future'

What you hear: 'We're never going to look at your CV again.'
What the recruiter means: 'We'll get back in touch if a suitable vacancy comes up, but we can't guarantee it.'

After hearing this, you're probably left wondering if they're telling the truth or just trying to spare your feelings. In reality, it could be a bit of both. And although they probably will keep your CV for future reference this doesn't mean that another relevant job will ever come up. Don't despair, though, it's not unknown for employers to approach unsuccessful applicants if the first round of interviews is disappointing, and you've nothing to lose by saying thank you and hoping for the best.

'We have a few more CVs to look at'

What you hear: 'We've already thrown you onto the reject pile.'
What the recruiter means: 'We have a few more CVs to look at.'

Sometimes, just sometimes, people do say what they mean. When you hear this, the best advice is to chill out and wait for them to come back to you. If you've still not heard anything after another couple of weeks, that's the time to follow up again.

WHAT DO YOU DO NEXT?

If this sounds like a lead-in to a motivational speech about not giving up, you're right. Becoming disheartened or taking it personally are the two most unproductive things you can do when you don't receive an invitation to be interviewed. There are plenty of inspiring examples to follow. J.K. Rowling's *Harry Potter* was rejected by 12 publishers before she landed a deal with Bloomsbury. Abraham Lincoln famously ran for Congress, the Senate, and the Vice Presidency five times before finally being elected President of the USA. Film director Steven Spielberg was turned down by the University of Southern California's School of Cinematic Arts three times before going on to make *Jaws, E.T.*, and *Raiders of the Lost Ark*. If motivation is what you need, you could do worse than pin this statement by top US basketball player Michael Jordan onto your wall:

> *'I have missed over 9,000 shots in my career.*
> *I have lost almost 300 games. On 26 occasions I have*
> *been entrusted to take the game-winning shot, and*
> *I have missed. I have failed over and over and over*
> *again in my life. And that is why I succeed.'*

Take every application as a learning experience and a sign that, no matter how prepared you may think you are, you can always make improvements. Whether it's checking the job description and requirements more carefully, asking someone to proofread your CV and cover letter, or tailoring your application more closely to the position, be sure to take something from it. After that, apply for your next job. Every time you improve your CV technique, you move yourself closer to the interview chair.

CHAPTER 11

The Top Five Don'ts and Dos

An added bonus of writing a winning CV is that you get to know yourself better. Putting yourself into a recruiter's shoes and viewing those fabled sides of A4 through their eyes can open the kind of window into your mind that you'd pay a therapist good money for. You also learn how to present yourself professionally on paper and online, at the same time as not erasing your personality or distinctive traits. This is powerful stuff for your career development.

You've discovered a lot, but let's take a moment to distil everything into five key dos and don'ts. These are the overarching principles of creating a CV that will gain a recruiter's attention in seven seconds or less, and they're the ones that you need to keep close to your heart at all times. It's not a bad idea to copy them out and put them by your keyboard while you write it.

THE TOP FIVE DON'TS

Don't be a generalist

If you're of a 'certain age', you'll remember when there were only two or three commercial TV channels in the UK, and the internet wasn't even a twinkle in Google's eye. In those prehistoric days, advertisers could broadcast mass messages to vast swathes of the population because none of us had much choice. Fast forward to now, and we're not satisfied with the broad-brush approach. If a company wants us to buy something, they'd better make us feel special or we're not interested. Marketers have caught onto that, and now segment their promotional messages much more tightly to the audience in question.

> 'Have an aim or objective. Can you convey to the reader what you're aiming to do? For example, "I am wanting to teach in further education and can see myself progressing in two years' time to running a department because I have x, y, and z skills."'

It's the same with your CV. If you give the same information to every recruiter, you'll run the risk of sounding generic. Actually, you might not even reach that far, because if they can't see instantly why you may be the best candidate for their particular opening they won't bother shortlisting you. They'll just reject you there and then. So tell the hiring manager up front why it's you they should consider, and back it up with facts and examples.

Don't forget your reader

When was the last time you started reading a book you hated, but managed to carry on to the bitter end? I wouldn't be surprised if it was never. We have a low tolerance for boring, confusing communications because they feel like a waste of time. CVs are a form of communication, so when you're writing yours take a little extra effort to consider your reader. Does it start in an attention-grabbing way? Would it inspire them to read on? Does it pack a punch? Sometimes, in the hours you spend crafting your CV, it's easy to forget that there'll be a human recipient at the other end who might be feeling tired, rushed, or uninterested. This leads nicely onto our next 'don't'.

*'For me, it's the punchy thing. You need short, snappy
bullet points to make it stand out.'*

Don't erase your personality

Job hunting can be a stressful process, and science has shown that when we feel under threat we often respond by retreating into our shells. From a biological standpoint, becoming invisible when you feel pressured makes sense, but it's a big mistake when you're out job hunting instead of big game hunting. Now's the time to make yourself visible, not to blend in.

'I didn't think "mediocre IT skills" was worth including.'

Think of some of your favourite and most successful media personalities. There won't be a bland one among them, and that's because we respond positively when we sense that we're in the presence of the real article rather than a made-up version with the rough edges smoothed out. Of course, if you're applying for a job as a retail assistant or an accountant, that's very different from wanting to be a TV star. But in the process of presenting yourself professionally, don't throw the baby out with the bath water by erasing all of your quirks and flaws – they're what make you believable and noticeable.

Don't forget that a job is a problem to be solved

Although it would be handy if they did, employers don't advertise job vacancies so they can pay people salaries, give them careers, and provide them with something interesting and useful to do all day. They do it because they have a collection of tasks and responsibilities that need taking care of. In other words, from an employer's perspective, a job is a problem to be solved. In fact, it goes further than that because their entire company exists in order to solve other people's problems. A clothing retailer solves the problem of how to look captivating on a Saturday night. An accountancy software developer helps small businesses to be more profitable. And a hospital solves the problem of poor health. Then, in order to achieve their objectives, these organisations generate yet more problems, which are what are known to you and me as jobs.

> *'Put what you achieved in your CV, not only your duties. Many candidates put their job description in there, but they don't tell you what they actually did in it.'*

To win with your CV, you need to show that you can solve that job problem better than the other candidates. If you forget that basic tenet of successful job hunting, you'll come across as someone who's only in it for themselves.

Don't lie

There's nothing wrong with highlighting your achievements in your CV – it is important for getting across your strong points. But there's a line to be drawn between that and stating or implying things that simply aren't true. Not only are you not doing yourself any long-term favours, but you'll also have a hard time convincing an interviewer that you're capable of the job. Worse, you're likely to have a horrible experience if you come to actually do it.

> *'A candidate left the review comments on his CV visible. One of the comments was, "I don't think you should lie about your academic background, they can find out."'*

There's a whole industry in producing fake qualifications. A company in Pakistan called Axact was found to be operating a network of hundreds of fake online universities, and they sold thousands of forged university degrees and qualifications.

Although purchasing a false qualification isn't a criminal offence in itself, using it in your CV when you apply for a job most certainly is. It's called 'fraudulent misrepresentation' and is punishable with up to ten years in prison.

At Reed we have a dedicated team of over 100 people purely to screen the CVs we receive, and we've found that 24 per cent of jobseekers have bumped up their results (turning a Third class degree into a 2:1 for instance). We even caught a candidate applying for a job as a social worker who had not only faked her qualification, but had lied about her registration with a professional body. Unsurprisingly, when we flagged this individual to the authorities we were told that she was already on their radar.

Usually, when candidates lie it's because they don't trust their skills, accomplishments, and personalities to win the interview. Don't make this mistake. The truth is, there's no need to do it. If you have a Third and you'd rather not mention it, just put BA Hons instead, and if you're asked about your grade come clean. Many employers realise that qualifications aren't everything – certainly some of the most successful people I know don't have top grades.

THE TOP FIVE DOS

Know your superpower

Understanding your talents and abilities and being able to connect them to the job you're applying for is the first step in creating a successful application. When you apply for a job that you have little ability or enthusiasm for, it shows. But when you know deep down that you can do it better than most of the other candidates, your strength transforms into a superpower and you become 'Super You'. This has a special effect: it attracts recruiters like a magnet, sending interview invitations to you just as quickly.

But your superpower only works if it's relevant for the role you're applying for, which brings us to the next 'do'.

Tailor your CV and cover letter

My work with recruiters shows time and again how much they value the candidates who have done their research, and tailored their CVs and cover letters accordingly. You know your super-power, so how does it relate to the job in question? By joining the dots for the hiring manager between your skills and experience, and the needs of the role, you'll be making it easy for them to say yes. It's so simple, and yet it takes an ability to see your CV through their eyes.

'Tailor your CV to the job description.'

It's easy to assume your CV should contain your whole career history, but that couldn't be further from the truth. Instead, pull out the achievements of your past that are most relevant to your future with that particular organisation. Show how you can be a problem solver in the context of your next job. What you've learned about tailoring in this book will help you to come across as impressive and unique. Don't blow that opportunity all for the want of an hour's online digging and a few meaningful tweaks of your CV – sometimes that's all it takes.

Prove your worth

Wouldn't it be so much easier if the recruiter just knew how great you were without you having to spell it out for them? 'Three years' experience as a retail assistant' – surely that should be enough, you think? Well, no. That's not only asking the hiring manager's brain to work overtime, but by expecting them to fill in the blanks you run the risk that they'll make the wrong assumptions. You'll also come across as lazy and unfocused.

'Anyone can write "I'm honest, reliable, and hard-working", but you need to prove that you have these qualities, for example: "I have experience in handling cash."'

The two key traits a recruiter looks for are competency and honesty. To show you're competent you need to be clear about your qualifications and your experience. What exactly did you achieve and for how long? Where do your particular strengths lie? And why should you be offered an interview, given the specifics you've mentioned? These are the solid details that will move you to the next stage because they're believable, credible, and trustworthy.

Be consistent, clear, and concise

The experience of job hunting was almost designed to be dispiriting. Writing endless CVs and cover letters, sending them off, waiting, praying, and then going through the whole cycle again can feel like a thankless task. But on the other hand pity the person who has to sift through hundreds of, often repetitive, applications. Imagine what it's like to come into work each day to a biblical flood of applications across a number of positions, and to have to compare them in double-quick time. It's a wonder a CV gets as much as seven seconds, let alone more. And it's no better for the 'non-professional' hiring manager who's looking to add to their team while juggling the recruitment process on the side.

'Be consistent with how you format your CV.'

So choose the right format and use plenty of white space. Being consistent with the way you present the information – would it be easy to read on a recruiter's phone as well as on their desktop? If your CV is hard to make sense of in terms of either content or presentation, it'll be dragged straight to the virtual trash bin.

> *'I had a CV once that contained the time of day the guy did particular things. I'm surprised it didn't have toilet breaks on there.'*

Check and check again

Employers don't want to hire people who are likely to make mistakes, and there's no easier way for them to draw the conclusion that you'll be error-prone than if your CV is littered with glitches. My research showed that the presence of spelling and grammar errors on a CV is the number two reason for it to land in the reject pile, and it's also a clear indication that an applicant isn't capable of paying attention to detail. This is incredibly easy to put right. The three simplest ways to spot mistakes are to ask a friend with an eye for detail to go through your CV, to read it backwards, and to check it in printed form. Also, try not to be in a rush. If you leave your work for a few days between writing and sending it off, you'll be more likely to spot the errors. Nobody gets it right first time, so don't expect that you will either.

> *'We did receive a CV in which someone referenced their "atention to detial". At least they nailed one out of the three words.'*

By now I hope you're convinced everybody can write a CV that impresses a recruiter within seven seconds of opening it, including you. It's not something that you can only achieve if you've got a top qualification, are a great writer, or are an expert in design software. All you need is some self-knowledge, a sensible way of organising your information, and the ability to communicate your worth so that your CV speaks instantly to the hiring manager who receives it. Now that you've discovered how to do this, you'll be fully equipped to land an interview for the job you dream of.

After all, seven seconds is all you need.

Good luck!

Once you've landed an interview as a result of your CV, your next step is to read my bestselling book *Why You? 101 Interview Questions You'll Never Fear Again*. It has helped countless jobseekers to secure the job of their dreams, because they were better prepared than the other applicants.

CV TEMPLATES

Please do make use of these templates, which have been created by Reed's dedicated career advice experts, to structure your CV. You'll find the classic reverse-chronological CV, the skills-based CV, and a series of sample CVs that are particular to your possible circumstances. These range from school leaver to graduate, career break to part-time and redundancy to career change. Explanations about which one to use for your own circumstances can be found in Chapters 2, 6, and 7. The wording in the templates is purely a guide – you must use your own to make your CV personal to you.

Alternatively, download our versions of these online, at www.reed.co.uk/career-advice/cvs/cv-templates.

REVERSE-CHRONOLOGICAL CV TEMPLATE

Name

Address

01234 000000 • 0113 000 0000 • name@mail.com •
www.linkedin.com/name

PERSONAL STATEMENT

A conscientious and professional personal assistant with extensive experience in administration, PA, and secretarial roles, currently seeking a new position as an Executive PA. A highly organised and efficient individual, whose thorough and precise approach to projects has yielded excellent results. Recent achievements with my current employer include the implementation of an innovative new filing and indexing system.

KEY SKILLS

- 80 words per minute typing
- Proficiency in all areas of Microsoft Office, including Access, Excel, Word, and PowerPoint
- Excellent communication skills, both written and verbal
- Accredited member of APA (Association of Personal Assistants)
- Fully qualified first aider

EMPLOYMENT HISTORY

PA to Personnel Manager, Company Name, Location
(April 2011 – Present)
Achievements and responsibilities:
- Implemented a change of stationery supplier, reducing costs by 20%
- Reorganised the meeting booking process, implementing an online system which all staff can access, leading to reduced diary conflicts within the team
- Devised and implemented a new filing and indexing system for files, resulting in greater ease of access and a more time-efficient process
- Helped provide a safer workplace by cataloguing and dispatching health and safety information and posters for the whole company
- Diary management, typing correspondence and documents, creating presentations, and creating meeting minutes

Front of House Receptionist, Company Name, Location
(June 2010 – April 2011)
Achievements and responsibilities:
- Presenting a professional and friendly first impression of the firm to all visitors and clients
- Managing incoming phone calls and mail

- Organising stationery orders and liaising with suppliers to meet business requests
- Replenishing and restocking the bar, always ensuring high level of stock management efficiency
- Also assumed the role of fire/health and safety officer for the entire office staff

Secretary, Company Name, Location
(October 2007 – May 2010)
Achievements and responsibilities:
- Maintaining and organising the company filing system
- Answering incoming calls
- Typing all necessary documents and correspondence as required
- Printing any supplementary notes as required
- Running professional errands

EDUCATION

College/School Name
(September 2004 – June 2006)
A-levels:
- General Studies – A
- English – B
- Mathematics – B

School Name
(September 1998 – June 2004)
10 GCSEs, grade A–C, including Maths and English

HOBBIES & INTERESTS

I am involved in a local amateur dramatics society, where I volunteer as a lighting and sound technician. I have been involved with this society for three years and very much enjoy being part of the team. More recently, I assumed the role of Stage Manager for a two-week production and relished the chance to take control of performances and react to a high-pressure environment.

REFERENCES

References are available upon request.

SKILLS-BASED CV TEMPLATE

Name

Address

01234 000000 • 0113 000 0000 • name@mail.com

PERSONAL STATEMENT

A Marketing graduate of (University Name), seeking a varied and challenging position that will consolidate my various types of experience. Knowledgeable about the fundamentals of marketing, along with business strategy, communication, and economic principles – as demonstrated throughout university and during part-time work. A motivated and creative self-starter with a comprehensive ability to meet deadlines, work well under pressure, and communicate effectively.

KEY SKILLS

Effective communication
- Able to communicate in a variety of ways, both verbally and orally – demonstrated in various presentations as well as seminar and lecture contribution
- Working in customer service has also helped me to build and expand on my communication skills. My role at (Company Name) involved daily interaction with all kinds of people.
- Confident communicator on a range of social media platforms – as shown when managing my university publication's social accounts

Creativity
- Skilled in generating creative ideas, and implementing them to meet strategic goals – as demonstrated during my time working a student journalist for the university newspaper
- Capable of producing aesthetically pleasing work, in a range of formats and media platforms – shown in a number of engaging presentations and projects that used a combination of text, imagery, and video

Commercial awareness
- Able to understand and utilise consumer behaviour in order to hit KPIs – as learnt in a number of modules, and in using my own blog to sell advertising space on a CPC basis
- Capable of measuring consumer behaviour by tracking various metrics, including page views, CTR, bounce rate, conversion rate, and search engine traffic
- Understand the importance of effective SEO practice and targeting when it comes to driving online traffic and increasing visibility
- Stay up-to-date with marketing trends – as shown with a recent project based around competitor insights and comparisons

IT & technology
- Intermediate user of Office applications, including Word, Excel, and PowerPoint.
- Abilities demonstrated in a range of university projects, as well as research and analysis tasks – using Google Analytics
- Competent user of Photoshop and Dreamweaver

EDUCATION

University Name
(September 2011 – July 2014)
Marketing (BA Hons) – predicted grade – 2.1
Core modules: Introduction to Accounting and Finance, Economic Principles for Business and Markets, Business Statistics, International Business Environment, Fundamentals of Marketing, Consumer Behaviour, Integrated Marketing Communications, Organisations and Management

College/School Name
(September 2009 – June 2011)
A-levels:
- Business Studies – A
- Maths – B
- Graphics – A

School Name
(September 2004 – June 2009)
10 GCSEs, grade A–C, including Maths and English

EMPLOYMENT HISTORY

Part-time Customer Service Assistant, Company Name, Location
(September 2011 – April 2012)
Achievements and responsibilities:
- Greeted and served customers in a polite manner, both in person and on the phone
- Rearranged promotional products to influence sales
- Encouraged 'bundle deals' and 'add-on products' to increase revenue and ensure customer satisfaction
- Replenished shelves within the set deadline in a neat and tidy manner, whilst rotating older stock to avoid wastage
- Ensured the shop was presentable

HOBBIES & INTERESTS

Avid blogger and social media user, and an owner of my own blog. Not only do I use it to write and edit articles about all topics related to sports (specifically football), I also use it as a platform to sell advertising space on a CPC basis. Whilst studying, I was also a member of my university football team, and contributed to the sports section in the student newspaper and social sites.

REFERENCES

References are available upon request.

SCHOOL-LEAVER CV TEMPLATE

Name

Address

01234 900621 • 0113 000 0000 • name@mail.com

Driving Licence • Own Car

PERSONAL STATEMENT

A highly motivated and hardworking individual, who has recently completed their A-Levels, and received excellent grades in both Maths and Science. Seeking an apprenticeship in the engineering industry to build upon a keen scientific interest and start a career as a maintenance engineer.

Mechanically minded, with a methodical approach to working and an eagerness to learn and develop personal skills in a practical setting. Eventual career goal is to become a fully qualified and experienced maintenance or electrical engineer, with the longer-term aspiration of moving into project management.

KEY SKILLS

- Advanced problem solving and numeracy skills
- Accomplished communication skills, both written and verbal, developed through numerous essays and presentations given during my time at college
- Ability to take the initiative and work well under pressure, ensuring strict deadlines are met, as successfully demonstrated during work experience placement project
- Flexibility, whilst maintaining enthusiasm and commitment to each project
- Proficiency in all areas of Microsoft Office, including Access, Excel, Word, and PowerPoint

EDUCATION

College/School Name
(2010 – 2012)
A-levels:
- Physics – A
- Maths – B
- Business Studies – B

School Name
(2004 – 2010)
10 GCSEs, grade A–C, including Maths (A) and Double Science (AA)

WORK HISTORY

Part-time Sales Assistant, Shop Name, Location
(April 2011 – Present)

Key results:
- Achieved four out of five revenue targets
- Personally billed over £10,000 since starting position.
- Demonstrated resilience and ability to upsell products, consistently meeting KPIs set for adding more value to sales.
- Significantly improved negotiation skills, regularly converting customers from point of enquiry to sale.

Pharmaceutical Company, Location *(unpaid work experience)*
(Summer 2009)
Duties included:
- Shadowed a key member of laboratory staff, observing their day-to-day work
- Spent a morning working within customer service centre, listening to client complaints and understanding company best practice when responding
- Assisted in project on risk management and contingency planning in case of failure at distribution centre
- Learned about company project management lifecycle methodology
- Gained knowledge of key health and safety standards used within the industry

HOBBIES & INTERESTS

Over the last two summers I have helped a family friend restore a classic sports car. This has triggered a passionate interest in mechanics and automotive restoration and, now that the project is finished, I have continued to build my knowledge by attending various classic car events.

During this time, I also decided to set up a blog around the project. Initially starting as a way to ask other collectors for advice whilst tracking progress, I began to enjoy writing about the subject and have now started writing occasional freelance articles for an online automotive magazine.

REFERENCES

References are available on request.

GRADUATE CV TEMPLATE

Name

Address

01234 900621 • 0113 000 0000 • name@mail.com

Driving Licence • Own Car

PERSONAL STATEMENT

A recent business economics graduate with a 2:1 honours degree from the University of X, looking to secure a Graduate Commercial Analyst position or similar to utilise my current analytical skills and knowledge and also help me to further develop these skills in a practical and fast-paced environment.

My eventual career goal is to assume responsibility for the analysis and implementation of all commercial data and actively contribute to the overall success of any business I work for.

EDUCATION

University Name
(2009 – 2012)
2:1 BSc. (Honours) Business Economics
Key skills gained:
- A keen international commercial acumen through applying economic theories and case studies to economies across the world
- Analytical and conceptual thinking, with a conscientious approach to managing workloads
- Ability to handle, analyse and interpret complex data, before presenting it back based on the overall analysis made
- Advanced problem solving and numeracy skills
- Accomplished communication skills, both written and verbal, developed through numerous essays and presentations
- Proficiency in all areas of Microsoft Office, including Access, Excel, Word, and Powerpoint

Notable Modules – Microeconomic & Macroeconomic Principles, International Economics, Econometric Methods & Applications, Financial Accounting & Statement Analysis

College/School Name
(2007 – 2009)
A-levels:
- History – A
- Business Studies – A
- Mathematics – B

School Name
(2001 – 2007)
10 GCSEs, grade A–C, including Maths and English

WORK HISTORY

Sales Assistant, Shop Name, Location
(April 2012 – Present)
Key results:

- Achieved four out of five revenue targets, equating to over 150% against overall targets set during entire period of employment
- Personally billed over £25,000 since starting position
- Demonstrated resilience and ability to upsell products, consistently meeting KPIs set for adding more value to sales
- Significantly improved negotiation skills, regularly converting customers from point of enquiry to sale, something which earned me Sales Assistant of the period during the month of June

Bartender, Bar Name, Location
(2010 – 2012)
Duties include:

- Serving customers in a polite and professional manner
- Replenishing and restocking the bar, always ensuring high level of stock management efficiency
- Helping train new team members in key competencies
- Demonstrating an in-depth knowledge of key health and safety standards used within the industry
- Managing heated incidences in a calm and professional manner.

HOBBIES & INTERESTS

I have a keen interest in photography. I was vice-president of the photography club during my time at university, and during this period I organised a number of very successful exhibitions and events both on and off campus.

I also play the piano to grade 8 standard.

REFERENCES

References are available on request.

CAREER-BREAK CV TEMPLATE

Name

Address

01234 000000 • 0113 000 0000 • name@mail.com

PERSONAL STATEMENT

A highly motivated and experienced PA, currently looking to resume my professional career after dedicating the last five years to raising a family. Excellent admin skills, thorough knowledge of all Microsoft Office programs, as well as proficiency in minute-taking and extensive experience liaising with clients. After volunteering for one day a week with a local charity to refresh my skills, now fully committed to continuing my career on a full-time basis.

KEY SKILLS

- Advanced typing skills (around 80 words per minute)
- Microsoft Office Specialist (MOS)
- Executive PA Diploma holder
- Experienced user of ICB Sage
- Qualified in both minute taking, and shorthand

EMPLOYMENT HISTORY

Voluntary Administrator, Company Name, Location
(January 2014 – Present)
Achievements and responsibilities:
- Typing correspondence
- Organising paperwork and filing documents
- Managing incoming post, and sending out any external mail
- Scheduling meetings between staff members
- Carrying out other administrative errands, including photocopying, faxing and ordering stationery

Career break taken to raise family
(2008 – 2013)

PA to Managing Director, Company Name, Location
(March 2004 – 2008)
Achievements and responsibilities:
- Provide administrative support to Managing Director
- Taking minutes during meetings with the board, which were then later typed and filed for easy access
- Represented the MD at any meeting she could not attend, and presented back all information gathered

- Full diary management, including booking meetings, event tickets, accommodation, transportation and flights efficiently, and within an annual budget of £5,000
- Organised and co-ordinated an annual training event for more than 50 members of staff
- Answering emails, incoming calls and running professional and personal errands to ensure MD could dedicate all available time to the business

Office Manager, Company Name, Location
(October 2002 – March 2004)
Achievements and responsibilities:
- Implemented a change of stationery supplier, reducing costs by 20%
- Reorganised the meeting room booking process, implementing an online system which all staff can access, leading to reduced diary conflicts within the team
- Devised and implemented a new filing and indexing system for documents, resulting in greater ease of access and a more time-efficient process
- Tracked office expenditure and prepared invoices
- Supervised all admin activities to ensure the office ran smoothly and efficiently

Office Administrator, Company Name, Location
(October 1997 – September 2002)
Achievements and responsibilities:
- Greeting up to 50 clients a day and presenting a professional and friendly first impression of the business to all visitors
- Managing incoming phone calls and mail
- Organising stationery orders and liaising with suppliers to meet business requests
- Carrying out other administrative errands including photocopying, printing, and faxing

EDUCATION

Executive PA Diploma
(April 2004 – January 2005)

College/School Name
(September 1995 – June 1997)
A-levels:
- English – B
- Mathematics – B
- Drama – C

School Name
(September 1990 – June 1995)
10 GCSEs, grade A–C, including Maths and English

REFERENCES

References are available upon request.

PART-TIME CV TEMPLATE

Name

Address

01234 000000 • 0113 000 0000 • name@mail.com

PERSONAL STATEMENT

An experienced Office Administrator, with over six years' worth of admin experience. Proven track record of success, including extensively improving efficiencies within my current organisation through the implementation of new indexing and filing systems. Also have a wealth of experience with regards to effectively liaising with multiple stakeholders around the business on a number of different projects.

Currently studying for my EA Diploma, and looking for a part-time position to complement my schedule. Extremely flexible with regards to working hours.

KEY SKILLS

- 80 words per minute typing
- Proficiency in all areas of Microsoft Office, including Access, Excel, Word, and PowerPoint
- Excellent communication skills, both written and verbal
- Highly adaptable, and able to pick up new systems quickly and efficiently
- Currently studying for an Executive Assistant Diploma

EMPLOYMENT HISTORY

Office Administrator, Company Name, Location
(April 2013 – Present)
Achievements and responsibilities:
- Implemented a change of stationery supplier, reducing costs by 20%
- Reorganised the meeting booking process, implementing an online system which all staff can access, leading to reduced diary conflicts within the team
- Devised and implemented a new filing and indexing system for files, resulting in greater ease of access and a more time-efficient process
- Helped provide a safer workplace by cataloguing and dispatching health and safety information and posters for the whole company
- Diary management, typing correspondence and documents, creating presentations, and creating meeting minutes

Admin Assistant, Company Name, Location
(June 2010 – April 2013)
Achievements and responsibilities:
- Maintaining and organising the company filing system
- Managing incoming phone calls and mail
- Organising stationery orders and liaising with suppliers to meet business requests

- Drafting email correspondence for senior management team
- Also assumed the role of fire/health and safety officer for the entire office staff

Secretary, Company Name, Location
(October 2009 – May 2010)
Achievements and responsibilities:
- Presenting a professional and friendly first impression of the firm to all visitors and clients
- Answering incoming calls
- Typing all necessary documents and correspondence as required
- Printing any supplementary notes as required
- Running professional errands

EDUCATION

College/School Name
(September 2007 – June 2009)
A-levels:
- Mathematics – B
- English – C
- Business Studies – C

School Name
(September 2001 – June 2007)
10 GCSEs, grade A–C, including Maths and English

HOBBIES & INTERESTS

I've been riding horses all my life, and I'm extremely passionate about all things equine. I've entered numerous competitions, where I've seen a great amount of success both local and on a county level, especially within dressage. I have been volunteering at a friend's stables for over four years, and recently helped organise a charity ball to raise money for maintenance and repairs – something which included designing and sending invitations, organising venues, and booking entertainment for the evening.

REFERENCES

References are available upon request.

REDUNDANCY CV TEMPLATE

Name

Address

01234 000000 • 0113 000 0000 • name@mail.com

PERSONAL STATEMENT

Driven Retail Manager with over ten years' experience in the fashion industry. Proven track record of success, including managing the top performing store in the region, and having the lowest staff turnover rate of all UK outlets. Currently out of work due to company closure, looking for the right opportunity to bring my expertise to a well-established fashion brand in an upper management position.

KEY SKILLS

- Excellent customer service skills
- Strong leadership skills, and the ability to motivate a successful team
- Expert knowledge of the fashion industry
- Experienced user of most sales software, including X, Y, and Z.
- Fully qualified first aider

EMPLOYMENT HISTORY

Manager, Company Name, Location
(January 2008 – December 2013)
Key results and responsibilities:
- Managed the top performing store in the South East
- Hit over 100% of revenue target in four out of five years
- Provided excellent working environment and employee morale, resulting in store achieving the lowest staff turnover of all UK outlets
- Attended numerous fashion shows and exhibitions to improve product knowledge, keep up-to-date in the industry and enhance the brand image
- Introduced new staff rota system and introduced overtime incentives, which in turn led to a 10% reduction in wage costs

Assistant Manager, Company Name, Location
(January 2006– January 2008)
Key results and responsibilities:
- Helped manage a team of 20 individuals
- Store nominated for local award recognising best customer service in our industry
- Team billed over £1,000,000 in one year for the first time in company history
- Wrote all course content for new starters, including product and sales training
- Promoted to 'Acting Manager' position when superior was on annual leave
- Oversaw all deliveries and managed stock control, wage budgets, and a number of other key management tasks

Sales Assistant, Company Name, Location

(April 2002– January 2006)

Key results:

- Achieved over 150% against overall targets set during entire period of employment
- Personally billed over £250,000 since starting position
- Demonstrated resilience and ability to upsell products, consistently meeting KPIs set for adding more value to sales
- Significantly improved negotiation skills, regularly converting customers from point of enquiry to sale, something which earned me Sales Assistant of the period for three consecutive months

EDUCATION

College/School Name

(September 2002 – June 2004)

A-levels:

- English – A
- Mathematics – B
- Business Studies – C

School Name

(September 1997– June 2002)

10 GCSEs, grade A–C, including Maths and English

REFERENCES

References are available upon request.

CAREER-CHANGE CV TEMPLATE

Name

Address

01234 000000 • 0113 000 0000 • name@mail.com

PERSONAL STATEMENT

As an experienced Sales Manager, my tenacious and proactive approach has resulted in numerous important contract wins. My excellent networking skills have continued to provide my team with vital client leads, and I've particularly excelled in developing client relationships – resulting in an 18% increase in business renewals for my current organisation.

I would now like to utilise these skills, as well as the experience gained from my eight years in sales, and undertake a new challenge as an Events Manager for an award-winning Marketing agency.

KEY SKILLS

- Advanced negotiation skills and experience dealing with big brands, including X, Y, and Z
- High level of focus on events management, both for team building and sales boosting purposes
- Excellent account management, resulting in an 18% increase in business renewals achieved in my current position
- Extensive experience allocating and managing six-figure budgets
- Highly adaptable in dealing with organisational change, demonstrated when having to provide cover for outgoing Manager in a neighbouring region
- Excellent management and team development skills

EMPLOYMENT HISTORY

Regional Sales Manager, Company Name, Location
(January 2015 – Present)
Achievements and responsibilities:
- Responsible for a team of 25 Sales Representatives
- Regional team achieved over £1million in revenue in a year for the first time ever
- Improved client relationships and increased sales through the organisation and implementation of various company-led lunch initiatives
- Increased annual profit margin by over 5% on previous year
- 18% increase in business renewals

Team Leader, Company Name, Location
(May 2010 – December 2014)
Achievements and responsibilities:
- Responsible for a team of ten Sales Executives
- Consistently achieved team targets, reaching 150% revenue against plan during whole period of employment

- Organised the company Christmas party on an annual basis, which helped to boost staff morale by X%.
- Designed and implemented a quarterly team-building event in order to improve communication, relationships, and goal alignment.
- Brought in a number of major new clients, including companies X, Y, and Z
- Attended a number of client meetings to ensure excellent account management was maintained
- Provided training, support and call coaching for new starters, as well as my own team members
- Extensively improved product knowledge, leading me to become the Sales Trainer for the whole South East region

Sales Executive, Company Name, Location
(July 2006 – May 2010)
Achievements and responsibilities:
- Hit my revenue targets for 12 consecutive periods
- Brought in £100,000 worth of new business during my time of employment
- Provided excellent account management to all clients, resulting in numerous testimonials
- Named Sales Executive of the Period on three separate occasions

EDUCATION

College/School Name
(September 2004 – June 2006)
A-levels:
- Biology – B
- Mathematics – B
- Sport Science – C

School Name
(September 1999 – June 2004)
10 GCSEs, grade A–C, including Maths and English

HOBBIES & INTERESTS

As a keen athlete, I spend a lot of my free time playing badminton – and have organised monthly tournaments within my local community for the past year. Not only did this involve finding venues and times that suited everyone, I also ensured refreshments were available for all participants. This helped boost numbers, and also increased overall club membership by 20% by the end of the year.

REFERENCES

References are available upon request.

COVER LETTER TEMPLATE

[Your Name]
[Address]

[Hiring manager's name]
[Hiring manager's company name]
[Company address]

[Today's Date]

[Name of Recipient]

Dear Mr/Mrs/Miss/Ms **[Hiring managers name – if not known, simply Sir/ Madam]**

I wish to apply for the role of **[Job Title],** currently being advertised on reed.co.uk. Please find enclosed my CV for your consideration.

As you can see from my attached CV, I have over **[Time period]** experience in the **[Sector]** industry, and I believe the knowledge and skills built up during this time make me the right/perfect candidate for the role.

In my current role as a **[Job title]** at **[Employer name],** I have been responsible for **[Insert a quantifiable and notable achievement/s – e.g. an x% increase in revenue]**, which when coupled with my enthusiasm and dedication **[Insert skills relevant to the role – usually found in the job description]**, has helped the business to **[Measure of success]**.

I am confident that I can bring this level of success with me to your organisation and help **[Company name]** build upon their reputation as **[State their position in market – learned through your research]**. With my previous experience and expertise, I believe my contribution will have an immediate impact on the business.

Thank you for your time and consideration. I look forward to meeting with you to discuss my application further.

Yours sincerely/Yours faithfully,
[Your name]
[Contact phone number]
[Signature – if desired]

Power Words

Sometimes it's hard to think of just the right word to turn your CV from mediocre to attention-grabbing, which is why so many people resort to obvious options. You can avoid your CV and cover letter becoming also-rans by using this list of power words for inspiration. They tap into recruiters' emotions, and lift the quality of your writing.

Words for leading

Inspired

Piloted

Spearheaded

Advanced

Headed up

Directed

Promoted

Motivated

Planned

Chaired

Pioneered

Led

Words for achieving

Attained

Reached

Executed

Fulfilled

Engineered

Gained

Won

Earned

Accomplished

Secured

Clinched

Completed

Obtained

Earned

Exceeded

Outperformed

Negotiated

Achieved

Words for creating

Innovated	Kindled
Generated	Engineered
Produced	Established
Designed	Initiated
Fostered	Introduced
Devised	Launched
Invented	Developed
Imagined	Created

Words for helping

Assisted	Advised
Alleviated	Coached
Supported	Consulted
Served	Moderated
Mitigated	Mediated
Encouraged	Helped

Words for improving

Increased	Outstripped
Decreased	Modified
Upgraded	Replaced
Enhanced	Reorganised
Boosted	Streamlined
Raised	Strengthened
Revamped	Updated
Tweaked	Transformed
Surpassed	Changed
Exceeded	Solved
Saved	Improved

Words for managing

Oversaw	Mastered
Organised	Aligned
Controlled	Mentored
Supervised	Recruited
Administered	Shaped
Handled	Trained
Influenced	Facilitated
Engaged	Managed

Words for analysing

Scrutinised	Measured
Surveyed	Evaluated
Examined	Tested
Calculated	Tracked
Explored	Interpreted
Identified	Analysed

Words for communicating

Liaised	Authored
Interacted	Campaigned
Wrote	Convinced
Transmitted	Documented
Persuaded	Promoted
Clarified	Designed
Reported	Briefed
Spoke	Communicated

Index

Acknowledgements

I would especially like to thank Ginny Carter, Max Dickson, Grace Donnelly, Laura Holden, and Rosie Reed for doing the 'heavy lifting' for this book; I could not have completed it without you. I would also like to thank my agent, Robert Smith; my editor, Carey Smith, and the team at Ebury for their editorial input. The research that was conducted to create the text was crowdsourced, as I described in Chapter 1, and it would not have been possible without the help and contributions from everyone listed below. Thank you.

Fiona-Grace Adams, Dan Addison, Yasmin Ahmed, Frank Ahmet, Rhys Aitchison, Jane Anderson, Holly Andrews, Mike Archer, Charlyne Asante, Callum Aston, Laura Backhouse, Iftikhar Bahakam, Christine Bailey, Michelle Ball, Veryan Barnes-Warden, Jonathan Barratt, Jacob Barron, Deanne Barthee, David Bartlett, Richard Bass, David Bass, Chelsea Battle, Darren Bayley, Tamina Becker, Claire Bedlow, Fiona Berry, Neil Bertman, Samina Bibi, Chloe Binns, Lindsay Blackman, Rebecca Blankenbyl, Deborah Blumfield, Jon Bolsover, Andreea Botu, Shaun Bourke, Lucy Bowdon, Stephanie Bowers, Elise Bowes, Mike Bowman, Claire Bowman, Stewart Boyd, Aislinn Brennan, Andrew Brennan, Craig Briddon, Laura Briggs, Paul Brogan, Heidi Brooks, Olivia Brown, Naomi Brown, Agnes Brown, Naomi Brown, Emily Bruce, Ross Bryant, Jacky Buchanan, Tom Bunkham, Luke Burdon, Taylor Burgen, Imogen Burgess, Mike Butler, Jake Butterly, David Button, Nick Caddy, Jeannie

Cain, Katie Cambray, Mark Canning, Lisa Cannonier, Tony
Carey, John Carr, Jane Cashmore, Jay Chamberlain, Michael
Cheary, Rosie Checksfield, Amanda Chick, Tony Child, Simon
Childs, Julie Chipp, Rebecca Chui, Rachel Clark, Heather
Clarke, Paul Clarke, Phil Clarke, Kate Clarke, Maryanne Clayton,
Nick Clement, Dawn Coady, Greg Cole, Tavis Coleman, Emma
Comben, Lisa Conlon, Rachel Connolly, Nicholas Connor, David
Constance, Jade Conway, Alex Cook, Toni Cook, Elizabeth Cook,
Ben Coppin, Paul Corcoran, Susie Corke, Claire Cornforth, Amy
Crawford, David Crichton, Thomas Cross, Francesca Crossley,
Thomas Crouch, Paul Crowther, Jade Cullen, Jade Cullen,
Jade Cullen, Mat Cummins, Martyn Cusack, Mark Cutts, Lacy
Dallas, Doug Dacre, Ryan Dalton, Adam Dasilva, Avgustina
Davidkova, Robert Davidson, Laura Davies, Gerwyn Davies,
Commie Dawson, Sue Dawson, Pat Deeley, Jason Dejonge, Dave
Demetriou, Richard DeNetto, Simone Devereux, Nicky Dick-
inson, Simone Donlon, Debbie Donnelly, Kevin Dorey, Annette
Doyle, Ross Drake, Dana Duma, Paul Dutton, Jack Eastwood,
Laura Eaton, Pamela Edwards, Derek Eelloo, Charlie Elgar,
Caroline Ellis, Katrina Ellis, Nicola Ellwood, Tracey English,
Lisette Etheridge, Irini Etimou, Annette Evans, Gareth Evans,
Matt Evans, Francesca Fallon, John Farmer, Alexandra Farrow,
Jane Faughnan, Ben Fellows, Vicky Fellows, Liz Fentiman, Kate
Ferguson, Aliyah Fernandez, Tracey Finch, Tony Finn-Ford,
Ralph Finnon, Richard Fisher, Lucy Flanagan, Ellise Fleming,
Clair Fleming, Jon Ford, Amy Foster, John Fraser, Russell Gale,
Dominic Gallagher, Matthew Gallivan, Sarah Giannotta, Andrew
Glass, Krista Godfrey, Pauline Godley, Daniel Gonzalez, Prav
Govender, Corissa Grech, Beth Green, Megan Greenslade, Ann
Gregson, Nichola Gudger, Natalie Hailey, Antony Hall, Mark
Hall, Natalie Hands, Jayne Hardman, Adam Harkin, Danielle
Harris, Sean Harrison, Sarah Hart, Craig Haward, Marcus
Headicar, Cristy Healey, Victoria Hearn, Erika Hemsworth,
Gavin Henson, Jon Herbert, Nicola Hewitt, Fran Higgins, Adam

Hiles, Racheal Hill, Christina Hinder, Sarah Hine, Jim Hoare, Daniel Hobbs, Cherie Hodder, Nicola Holdaway, Jack Holden, Becky Hole, Peter Holmes, Jolene Hopkinson, Will House, Sophie Howard, Tracy Howard, Natalie Hudson, Nick Hughes, Joseph Hughes, Eleanor Hughes, Hannah Hughes, Jenny Hulcoop, Dan Hunter, Opeyemi Hussain, Dawn Hyslop, Arslan Iqbal, Nick Ison, Andrew Jackson, Harriet Jacobs, Catherine James, Ryan Jones, Lee Jones, Darren Jones, Denise Jones, Marianne Jones, Rohan Kallicharan, Louise Keegan, Dione Keen, Sumayah Khan, Phil Kidd, Tim King, Louise Kingham, Elsa Knight, Sam Koroglu, Monika Korycka, Calvin Krause, Rakesh Kripalani, Rob Lamb, Zuleika Lambe, Laura Langley, Sameena Laskar, John Latham, Richard Latus, Graham Leach, Helen Lee, Alison Lees, Karen Legett, Rebecca Leggatt, Chris Legge, Paul Lenzan, Chloe Lewis, Jenni Lewis, Ian Lewis-Johnson, Annabeth Limb, Simon Lincoln, Annette Lind, Francesca Lloyd, Holly Lyall, Joey Lynch, Niall Mackenzie, Romaana Mahtey, Keith Malin, Claire Maltby, Maria Margariti, Greg Martin, Jane Massey, Carl Maw, Holly McCauley, Chloe McConnell, Steven McCormick, Margaret Mcgeever, Cameron Mckay, Kerry Mcne, Tanya Meah, Brendan Megaw, Richard Merkl, Shuhel Miah, Amy Middleton, Tom Millar, Natalie Minshall, Antonio Miragliotta, Harpreet Mitchell, Anouska Mond, Jo Moore, Joshua Moore, Denise Moran, Jon Moreline, Isabella Mori, Yoko Morinaka, Sally Morley, Jill Morley, David Morris, Kath Morrison, Lucy Mullen, Yve Murphy, Paul Murphy, Anita Nadkar, James Nathan, Alexa Naylor, Tony Neagen, Linda Neal, Kelly Neath, Christopher Nevin, Tim Newman, Kelly Nicholls, Andrew Nicholson, Danielle Nicholson, Phillipa Nicholson, Mel Nield, Jeanette O'Connell, Becky O'Hanlon, Helena O'Keeffe, Debbie O'Neill, Sally O'sullivan, Ian Ochtman, Ella-Marcelle Olamiju, Christopher Olashore, Damien Ollerhead, Steve Othen, Jenny Otoo, Gabriel Ozique, Lucia Pace, Kelly Page, Simon Pagram, Jonathan Palmer, Kathryn Papworth-Smith, Sarah Parker, David Parker, Sarah Parnell, Linda Parry,

Meera Patel, Vanessa Payne, Marcos Pearson, Lizzie Peck, Robert Pegg, Shelley Pegg, David Penlington, Rhsy Penny, Rachael Penycate, Andrew Pettingill, Steve Philcox, Sharon Phillips, Jon Philo, Robert Pick, Emma Sarah Piorkowski, Timothy Pool, Sagar Popat, Chris Porter, Delfin Posada, Dominik Potworowski, Sara Poulton, Susan Pow, Alex Powell, Sophie Preston-Hall, Christine Price, Samantha Price, Adam Pudvine, Sara Pugh, Anna Pullen, Bev Pullin, Suzanne Ramsay, David Randall, Danielle Randall, Kelly Randall, Sunit Ravaliya, Andrea Raven-Hill, Jon Ravenhall, Nicola Reed, Sir Alec Reed, Andrew Reeves, Adam Reynolds, Mark Rhodes, Luke Richardson, Leigh Richardson, Debbie Ridgett, Paul Ridley, Ian Roberts, Karl Roberts, Michael Roberts, Harry Roberts, Charlotte Robertson, Ed Robinson, Reece Rochester, Jasmine Rogers, Amber Rolfe, Matthew Rolfe, Lynne Rose, Graeme Ross, Joanne Rowbotham, Elizabeth Rowe, Kristy Rowlett, Louise Rushton, Andy Ryan, Maryam Sadeghi, Robb Sands, Eleanor Schader, Mark Scott, Rebecca Sell, Jeff Sharma, Rebecca Shaw, Chris Shaw, Christine Shervington, Amanda Shoyer, Deborah Sibley, Sharan Sidhu, Kerry Simms, Jo Simpson, Aditi Singh, Bruce Sleap, Lisa Smith, Jodi Smith, Dale Smith, Ashley Smith, Andrea Smith, Mark Smith, Sam Smitten-Downes, James Soden, Suzie Solly, Tanya Sones, Simon Spencer-Rouen, Donne Stam, Will Stanley, Jen Stapleton, Lewi Steadman, Izabella Stechman, Matthew Steedman, Roni Steptoe, Mark Stewart, David Stickings, Kellie Stones, Kelly Strong, Anjulie Sudhir, Adele Taggart, Luca Tajti, Dan Tanner, Emily Taper, Daniel Telfer, Mel Telford, Claire Temple, Jonathan Thelwell, Gareth Thomas, Mara Thorne, Lisa Townsend, Laura Trought, Gavin Tufton, Elizabeth Turner, Elizabeth Turner, Paul Turner, Michael Turville, Angela Tuvi, Claire Tyler, Pam Underwood, Rositsa Velikova, Matthew Venables, Nigel Venables, Lizzie Verbeek, Kay Vorley, Myna Vu, Emma Wadding, Beren Walker, Sue Walker, Jessica Walton, Carys Ward, Ben Ward, Francesca Webb, Hannah Weeks, Katie Weller, Marie Weston,

Olivia Whitaker, Harriet White, Katie Whiteway, Deirdre Wilcock, Ken Wilkins, Stephen Wilkinson, Margaret Wilkinson, Caroline Wilkinson, Courtney Williams, Karen Williams, Sue Williams, Luke Williams, Colin Willsher, Sarah Wilson, David Wilson, Simon Wingate, Francisco Wingrove, Amanda Wise, Charlotte Witchard, Allison Worley, Michelle Wright, Graham Wyllie, Ally Yates, Heather Young.

If you have submitted a CV recently and there are specific rules for your sector that I haven't mentioned in this book, please email me at james@reed.com or tweet using #7SecondCV and tell me about your CV experiences. Your help will be greatly appreciated and will make future editions even more definitive.